P9-CNI-769

CHILDREN & SCISSORS

A DEVELOPMENTAL APPROACH

Patricia Buerke Moll, M.A.

Hampton Mae Institute, Tampa, Florida

Photographs by
Simon's Studios

Book Design by
Mary Floyd

Third Edition

First Edition printed July 1975

Second Edition
1st printing October 1985
2nd printing November 1986

Second Edition - Revised
1st printing July 1987
2nd printing October 1988

Third Edition
1st printing March 1995

ISBN 0-9616511-7-2 Perfect Binding   ISBN 0-9616511-6-4 Spiral Binding

Copyright 1985, 1995 by Patricia Buerke Moll, 4104 Lynn Avenue, Tampa, Florida 33603

All rights reserved. No part of this book may be reproduced or utilized in any form or by any means, electronic or mechanical, including photocopying, recording or by any information storage or retrieval system, without permission in writing from Patricia Buerke Moll, 4104 Lynn Avenue, Tampa, Florida 33603.

Please address your ideas and comments to Patricia Buerke Moll, M.A., Hampton Mae Institute, 4104 Lynn Avenue, Tampa, Florida 33603

The eye screening list on page 108 is adapted from Garwood S. Gray's **Educating Young Handicapped Children** (1979) by permission of the publisher, Aspen Systems Corporation.

Dedication

WILMA CLARK FOYE
"Thanks, Billie"

In Memoriam

ELLEN THIEL, M.A.
JEANNE RYAN, Ph.D

ACKNOWLEDGMENTS

Books are a joint effort. They require the persistence, intelligence, self-discipline, encouragement, criticism, and guts of many people. When these efforts are finally honed into a tangible object, the author's feelings of gratitude to those who helped are rightly expressed in the acknowledgments.

Ellen Thiel, M.A. and Jeanne Ryan, Ph.D., at Florida State University gave me the educational philosophy foundation which is responsible for the child-oriented format of <u>Scissors</u>. I hope they will be pleased to recognize it as another fruit of their labor: reaching out to help children.

Fellow educators who cajoled, inspired, criticized, contributed ideas, activities and shared their children and classrooms should also be thanked by the rest of you who will reap the rewards of their input when you use this book. We thank Cathy Battle, Ph.Ed; Barbara Bradley Buerke, Dorothy Buerke, Jean Chichester, Lillian DeWilz, Kitty Getz, Virginia Gusham, Evelyn Johnson, Emma Hendrix, Ruby Presley, Rosetta Todd, Frances Worden, Ruby Wright and participants in my Scissoring Workshops.

A special thanks also to Patricia Holmes, Jeanette Rush and their kindergarten children for their patience with me while I learned about scissoring.

Mary Bennett and Billie Foye spent many hours with me, reading, talking, and listening. The quality of this material is a reflection of their concern for helping each child to grow at an individual rate.

So many children played a vital role in the development of <u>Scissors</u> it is impossible to name them all. So these few will represent the others: Bob, Katie and Natalie Buerke, Amanda Colla, Camilla and Ean Church, Nicole Cuddleback, Jonathan and Jeremy Davis, Billy Jordan, Taneshia and Jabari Judge, Heather Khan, Bobby McConnell, Angela and Melissa Newkirk, Lenill and Mark Roccaforte, Gabriel and Greg Salmon, Kimberly Dawn Tangunan, Cherese and Kameelah Timmons, Marisa Scalera, Chris and Jason Dickey, Jennifer Miller and Heather Vance.

Fortunately, I found several people who could take the pieces of my rough draft and puzzle and type them into copy. Thanks Martha Almquist, Gloria Clark, Anne Everett and Margaret Peeler.

The photography in this book certainly illustrates the adage "a picture is worth a thousand words." You can thank the patience and persistence of Simon Rose for these photos. We spent many an hour setting up, retaking and reprinting until he was satisfied with their clarity.

Credit should also be given to photographer George Salmon, who first taught me what the camera can see.

Thank you, Mary Floyd, for being my "expert" on getting it all together into book form.

The last leg of this production was completed by M & M Printing Co., Inc. in Ruskin, Florida. I thank them for hanging in there with me: especially Celeste Buzbee, who took the final puzzle and set it into readable type.

Patricia Buerke Moll
October 7, 1985

P. S. Nice to have you join the caravan.
RHB, Old Lady and Magoo

FIRST EDITION

ACKNOWLEDGEMENTS

Third Edition

This book continues to grow in its reflection of children's needs and expression because of all of you who send questions and comment on its content. Thank you to all the workshop participants, the letter writers, and those who took the time to make comments. Please keep the comments and questions coming.

The new children's faces which appear in this edition belong to: Aramita Wingate, Jahmal Douglas, Terry Morre, Breanna Evans, Thomas Feleciano, Christopher Feleciano, Danielle Colla, Kimyetta Moore, Cartaya Moore, Kristy Heeter, Lauren Shackton and Jermaine Gosa. Their art work and the art work of Brenda Flicker and Sarah Barry's kindergarten classes, my Pre-K class at Lockhart Elementary, and the 5 and 6 year olds at the Evans Center will show what children "really do" with scissors.

Emily Fraiser has given her support and encouragement to this project for many years. Brenda Flicker, Cathy Cantanna, Trudy Palmer, Donna Taber and Linda McNeil represent all of you who have continued to give me your success stories and serve as a catalyst for me to do more books.

Final thanks goes to Wilkinson & Associates and to Janet Lynne Woods for our new look.

Patricia Buerke Moll
March 14,1995

P. S. Still a full caravan! Alaska here we come!

CONTENTS

Chapter Five
Line Cutting Sequence

Chapter One

Readiness

For Learning
The Art
Of Cutting

A child learns each new skill when his total self is ready to learn that particular skill. That is to say, his mental, physical, neurological, and psychological selves must be totally integrated and developed to the levels required to approach that particular learning situation. So it is with scissoring.

Thus, before beginning to help a child learn to cut, a review of the child's overall skill level is necessary.

Informal observation of the child during routine activities can give clues to her readiness for scissoring.

This chart gives an informal organization of usual activities found in your classroom on a daily basis. It also shows that learning is a continuing process, and so what the child is ready for today is a result of his past experiences. The activities are familiar to you. For common agreement, the areas of developmental growth are defined as follows:

1. Knowledge of body parts:

a. Identification of body parts by verbally labeling them and by appropriately identifying them when given a verbal label.

b. Identification of position of the part on the body (understands hand and arm go together, parts of the face, etc.).

c. Identification of parts related to their position in space: head above shoulders as highest parts, (e.g., moving forward or backward, which part leads, etc).

d. Identification of body part functions: what each part does.

e. Activities which allow the child to establish dominance (e.g., eating, reaching, throwing, holding, squeezing, kicking, climbing stairs, etc.).

2. Bilateral integration:

Activities which require that the two sides of the body work together (e.g., crawling, walking, running, catching and throwing, swimming, swinging, etc.).

3. Use of hands:

   a. UNILATERAL - one hand is required to do the job.
   b. RECIPROCAL - both hands are required to do the task, and each hand is doing the same task.
   c. BILATERAL - both hands are required to do the task, and each hand is performing a separate task for the common outcome.

4. Prehension:

Development of one of the kinds of hand grasps.

5. General motor development:

Fine and/or gross motor movement of hand and/or body.

6. Eye-hand coordination:

The eyes and hands working together at levels of both fine and gross motor coordination.

Note: For further help with an understanding of areas 1-6, read material on perception and motor movement education (see Further Readings).

7. Language:

Receiving and using those words which are essential to understanding the verbalization of the art of cutting.

Language experience is one of the most important areas of developmental growth with young children. Cutting is an excellent avenue for development of language. It is essential that the children come to the activity with preparatory language. An absence of this "pre-cutting language" complicates the skill unnecessarily. Help your children to develop a correct usage of cutting words before attempting to teach them to cut, and further expand their language by having them use these words when talking about their projects.

The chart is a guide to readiness activities for cutting and an informal check list of the skills necessary for learning to cut. A lack of experience with these activities could mean a lack of the hand strength and coordination required to manipulate the tool.

2

Teacher Ideas

Note: Most of you are aware of developing closing strength. Remember opening strength as well. Scissoring is a two -handed skill. Be sure to provide activities which require the use of both hands. Each hand should be performing a different movement or action.

1. Plastic bucket full of sponge pieces: the child takes out and puts in the pieces using kitchen tongs. Move to solid objects to continue to develop strength and coordination.
2. Puppet with a movable mouth (opening strength).
3. Screw tops on and off plastic bottles: not child resistant type (two hands, each hand has a different job: bilateral integration).
4. Any of the activities listed in the chart on pages 4 and 5.

COORDINATING AREAS OF DEVELOPMENTAL GROWTH AND ACTIVITIES

ACTIVITY	Knowledge of Body Parts	Bilateral Integration	Use of Hands	Prehension	General Motor Development	Eye-Hand Coordination	LANGUAGE
thumb sucking	•			•	G		
rolling over	•	•			G		
reaching, grasping	•	•	•	•	G	•	normal mother-child talk
extending index finger	•		U	•	F		
waving "bye-bye"	•	•	U		G		
holding objects	•	•	•	•	F	•	hand — hold
self-feeding hand & spoon	•	•	•	•	•	•	thumb — give
crawling	•	•	•	•	G	•	down — here
pulling up	•	•	R,B	•	G	•	up — tight
sitting	•	•	R,B		G		finger — squeeze
hugging	•		R,B		G	•	sit
clapping	•	•	R,B		G	•	in
releasing an object	•	•	•	•	•	•	out
finger painting	•	•	•	•	•	•	
squeezing foam	•	•	•	•	•	•	
climbing	•	•	•	•	•	•	squeeze — paper
pulling objects	•	•	•	•	•	•	point — open
steering on ride toys	•	•	•	•	•	•	pick-up — close
patty-cake	•	•	•	•	•	•	put down — hold
squeezing water out of things	•	•	•	•	•	•	take — line
screwing tops on plastic bottles	•	•	•	•	F		pointer — fingers
finger plays	•	•	•	•	•	•	trigger — walk
swinging	•	•	•	•	•	•	tall man — take
walking line	•	•	B	•	•		middle finger — thumb
jungle gym	•	•	•	•	G	•	stop — arms
rope swing	•	•	•	•	G	•	go — eyes
naming body parts	•	•	U,B	•	•	•	on — head
string pull on talking toys	•	•	B	•	•	•	rest — top
painting (brush)	•	•	U	•	•	•	tear — bottom

4

LEGEND

Use of Hands

U - Unilateral
R - Reciprocal
B - Bilateral
• - All of U,R,B

General Motor Development

G - Gross
F - Fine
• - Both G & F

COORDINATING AREAS OF DEVELOPMENTAL GROWTH AND ACTIVITIES

ACTIVITY	Knowledge of Body Parts	Bilateral Integration	Use of Hands	Prehension	General Motor Development	Eye-Hand Coordination
hopping	•	•	B		G	
skipping	•	•	B		G	
jump rope	•	•	•	•	G	•
ball play	•	•	•	•	G	•
multiple food utensil use	•	•	•	•	•	•
buttoning	•	•	R,B	•	•	•
playdough	•	•	•	•	•	•
shaking hands	•		V	•	G	•
tweezers	•	•	U,R	•	F	•
food tongs	•	•	U,R	•	•	•
sorting small items	•	•	•	•	F	•
pick-up sticks	•	•	•	•	F	•
sew & lacing activities	•	•	•	•	•	•
peg boards, nail board	•	•	•	•	•	•
tracing	•	•	•	•	•	•
bead stringing	•	•	•	•	•	•
squeeze-type clothes pins	•	•	R,B	•	F	•
finger painting	•	•	•	•	•	•
screw board	•	•	•	•	•	•
taffy pull	•	•	•	•	•	•
rhythm activities	•	•	•	•	•	•
spreading jam on bread	•	•	U,B	•	•	•
hole punch	•	•	•	•	F	•
blocks	•	•	•	•	•	•
pasting and gluing	•	•	•	•	•	•
tearing paper	•	•	R,B	•	•	•
cutting	•		B	•	•	•

LANGUAGE

across	straight
along	tear
circle	front
square	back
corner	here
open-close	there
to	other
toward	another
off	the
on	move
hole	part
shut	hard
right	guide
left	slow
start	slowly
paste	
glue	
spread	
around	
into	

scissors	fringe
blades	snip
chew	slip
cut	

LEGEND

Use of Hands

U - Unilateral
R - Reciprocal
B - Bilateral
• - All of U,R,B

General Motor Development

G - Gross
F - Fine
• - Both G & F

Chapter Two

Gluing
And
Tearing Skills

Gluing is a separate skill that children need to master before they begin learning the complex skills of cutting. As shown on the growth and development chart, gluing helps to develop all of the areas which are required for learning to cut. It is a necessary pre-scissoring skill.

The use of the word glue as opposed to paste, is intentional. There are two reasons for the preference of white glue to paste. First, when children use glue on a project, it will stay glued and not fall apart. This shows the children that you value their work enough to insure its permanency. Secondly, white glue is easier for young children to spread.

If you are committed to paste, here is a suggestion to make it work better. Be sure the children completely cover whatever they are pasting. This will insure a complete bond. It is the air spaces that dry up the paste. When the paste dries up and cracks, the project falls apart.

This author has learned of a new concoction from a participant in a workshop . You can call it "glaste" or "plue." Combine 2/3 white paste to 1/3 white glue and beat until creamy. The measurements are not exact. You want a mixture like whipped cream. It will spread easily and keep the bondability of glue. It will mildew, so mix up only what you need for about a week. It can be placed on a scrap of paper like paste, so that each child has her own "plue." This concotion is appropriate for most projects. Glitter, leaves, items from nature walks, and cloth may still require white glue.

A recent product on the market is "gel;" it dries faster than glue and comes in a squeeze bottle. The reports of its use from classrooms is positive, although some children do have difficulty squeezing the "gel" out of the bottle.

Remember that young children are learning through their senses. They are going to want to know how the glue tastes, especially if you mix the glue and paste while the children are watching. You should decide ahead of time whether tasting will be permitted in your classroom. One taste will be enough for most of the children. A few will have to remind themselves of its taste for the first few activities. When the children know how glue tastes, they will then be glad to use it for its designated purpose, and not spend their time trying to sneak a taste.

You may have a child who likes the taste of the glue and will want to eat it. Those of you who use paste should be aware that some school paste has a peppermint taste. Children who enjoy eating the glue can be looked at in several ways. As long as no issue is made by the child, then eating small amounts may not be harmful and could be ignored (**you decide for your classroom**). Telling the child that glue is for gluing, not a food, may be helpful. Your children will be eager to say "yuck, you don't eat paste." If the child persists in eating the glue, talk to the parents. A persistent eating of the glue could indicate a nutritional need, a metabolic imbalance, and/or an emotional disturbance. So consider these possibilities when you have a child who eats large quantities of glue or paste.

Starting with gluing, you have an opportunity to teach the child how to organize a work area. When you get to scissoring, it will be a great help to the children if they are in the habit of having an organized work area.

Talk with your children about the organization of the work area, and be sure that they have enough table space in which to work. The child's work space should be at least 30 inches by 30 inches. The height of the work space should be below the level of the child's elbow. This allows the child comfortable use of his hands. You decide whether children may stand while working the art area in your classroom, and particularly if the may stand and walk while holding scissors.

The following arrangement of materials has been found to be very successful. The background area or the piece to be glued on, goes directly in front of the child. A small amount of "glaste" is placed on a piece of scrap paper, along with a paper towel or wet cloth for wiping glaste off of his hands. These should be placed on the child's non-dominant side. This requires the child to reach across his mid-line each time he wants to glue. Crossing the mid-line is a valuable pre-reading exercise. Then on the child's dominant side place the pieces to be glued.

Other considerations should include where children will work and which children will sit next to each other.

Deciding on the children's individual spaces before the activity begins will head-off social-interaction problems during the activity. Some children require a lot of space in which to work. Their work seems to take on a life of its own. Their paper pieces, glue and scissors tend to move into other children's spaces. Conflict then arises over ownership of pieces. "Teacher, Terry messed up my paper" is frequently heard.

Talk to "Terry," who needs more space, before you start the activity. Help find a space, perhaps a table for "Terry," where "Terry" can work without conflict. By making these arrangements at the start of the activity, you are telling "Terry" "I understand your needs and want you to have a happy, productive time with these materials". While waiting until the conflict arises puts "Terry" in the position of again being in someone else's space without being invited. Usually "Terry" will have a friend who does not mind "Terry's" materials mixed with her own.

Mark Terry's space in some way. Use masking tape, a different colored paper to cover his space, some visual clue to help Terry identify the boundaries of Terry's work area. This will help Terry to learn to limit the space needed for Terry's materials.

You may want to cover the entire work area with newspaper.

Now that the work area is organized, and everyone has decided glue is not for eating, we are ready to begin gluing. Have the child bring the piece to be glued to the glue. By placing the piece to be glued on the paper towel, the child will learn to contain the messiness.

Otherwise, the child will have long streams of white glue all over the project. An advantage of white glue is that a little bit goes a long way. Encourage the children to use only a "little bit" of glue. The "glaste" concoction makes it easier for the child to control the amount of "glaste" she is using for her project. Teach the child to use only one finger for gluing. Then show the child how to pick up the glued piece and put it in place with his clean fingers. This helps to build strength and coordination in these fingers.

Your children are at a tactile stage in learning. The use of paint brushes, popsicle sticks or fingers is an individual teacher's decision. We use fingers in our classroom. Children need to learn that they can use their hands and control messiness. Given ample opportunity to fingerpaint, children will be more willing to use the "glaste" to put their projects together, rather than to use the "glaste" to fingerpaint. With your step-by-step instruction, they can learn to control the materials. This process will be a rewarding experience for them and for you.

When you feel your children have gluing well under control, then it is time to teach tearing.

Tearing also has a sequence of skills and appropriate language to be taught.

A child's first attempts at tearing begin at about the age of two, when her hands can perform a reciprocal task (a task where each hand is performing the same task at the same time). Next the child is ready to make a bilateral tear (where one hand pulls away from the body and the second hand pulls toward the body).

Use a variety of papers in your tearing activities. Most paper has a grain. That means it will tear straight in one direction and ragged in another direction. Take a piece of newspaper and tear it from top to bottom. Did it tear straight? Tear it from side to side. Did it tear ragged? The straight tear is "with the grain." That is the way you want to give it to your children to tear when they are first learning to tear. Older children should be taught the language and given the opportunity to discover the grain of many kinds of paper.

Always test the qualities of the papers (i.e., direction and ease of tearing) before you give them to your children. Then be creative and give your children other things to tear also, such as lettuce, old cloth, playdough, leaves, etc. (**Be sure to check for non-toxic contents.**)

Separate the tearing and gluing activities when working on a project. First complete all of the tearing, then reorganize for gluing. You may even want to tear on one day and glue on the next.

Instructions for teaching tearing skills will be as follows:

1. A new skill will be introduced. Instruction will be given to the teacher for presentation to the child, and observation of skill development. Instructions for the left-handed child mirror those for the right-handed child.

2. Problems which may arise are listed and some solutions are given. Reference is made as to which developmental task from Chapter 1 should be provided to enhance developmental growth when required.

3. Activities are structured so that the children will become used to an organizational pattern for doing these activities. The organized child will then be able to use his energies on creativity within each activity, as he develops expressive language and visual perceptions of his world. The project directions are for the teacher's comfort level. Please note that the structure serves to give the child a sense of order to her work, NOT to dictate how each piece should be placed on the project. Helping the child to order her world allows her the freedom to express her creativity on each project. Remember, after you give the child the paper pieces they belong to her. She should decide how she wants to place them on her paper. Believe in her development and help her be proud of her present skill level.

Always have extra pre-cut pieces as well as your scrap box available for your children. This encourages them to make their own decisions about how their project should look.

Note: Each child should be given the option of not choosing any particular "project." She should be able to create her own ideas or move on to another activity in the classroom. Do continue to encourage children to tear paper for their projects. They need the experience for pre-writing development.

9

Reciprocal
Tearing Motion

I. Instructions

A. Skill
Hands pull away from the mid-line to make tear.

B. Language

tear	pull	pop	rip
both	hands	apart	grab

C. Materials
Newspaper strips, 1" x length of page (be sure to tear it with the grain.)

D. Procedure
1. Hands grab strip.
2. Hands pull in opposite directions, away from the mid-line (reciprocal motion).
3. Paper strip is popped into two pieces.

II. Problem and Solutions

Child cannot pull the paper apart.
1. Make the strip more narrow.
2. Use a lighter weight paper.
3. Return to other uses of hands and bilateral integration activities to build hand strength and coordination.
4. Test paper for grain.
    a. Establish top, bottom and sides for page. Tear top to bottom then tear side to side. Determine ease of tearing. Tearing with the grain is easiest.
    b. Cut strips to tear with the grain.

Headband

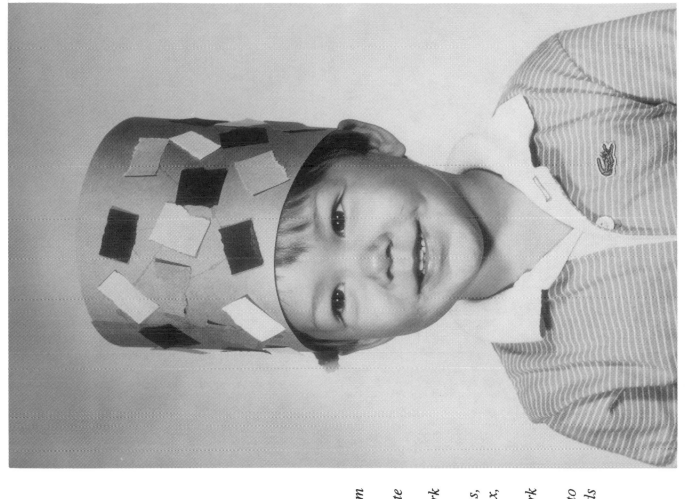

Supplies

Glue
Paper Towels
Stapler
Scrap Box

Teacher-Prepared Materials

4 Paper Strips, 1" x 12"
Paper Strip, 6" x 24"
   (Child's name on back.)

Procedure

1. Small group discussion.
a. Talk about and demonstrate the steps of making a headband.
b. Be sure the children understand they can make anything they would like to make.
c. Talk about and demonstrate how to tear the strip.
d. Pass out paper strips to be torn.

2. Child tears the 1" x 12" strip into pieces of varied length. (Some children may want to tear and not glue.)

3. Child may choose items from the scrap box.

4. Talk about and demonstrate how to use the glue.

5. Teacher sets up child's work area for gluing.

6. Child glues torn paper pieces, and a piece, from the Scrap Box, on 6" x 24" paper strip.

7. Child helps to clean up work area.

8. Teacher fits Headband to child's head and staples ends together.

Class Flag Display

Supplies

Glue
Paper Towels
Stapler
String
Scrap Box

Teacher-Prepared Materials

4 Paper Strips, 1" x 12"
Paper Rectangle, 6" x 9" (Child's name on back.)
Variety of shapes approximately 6" x 9" (Child's name on back.)

Procedure

1. *Small group discussion.*
a. Talk about flags and demonstrate how to make a Flag.
b. Ask for other ideas for things to make.
c. Talk about and demonstrate how to tear the strip.
d. Pass out paper strips to be torn.

2. *Child tears the 1" x 12" strips.* (Allow children to change activities if they have no interest in gluing.)

3. Talk with children about, and demonstrate how to use, the glue.
4. *Teacher sets up child's work area for gluing.*
5. *Child glues scrap pieces and torn paper pieces on 6" x 9" shapes.*
6. *Child helps clean up work area.*
7. Talk with children about how their flags and their shape designs can be displayed in the classroom.

Butterfly

Supplies

Glue
Paper Towels
Newsprint
String
Iron
Scrap Box

Teacher-Prepared Materials

4 Tissue Paper Strips, 1" x 12"
2 Waxed Paper Butterfly Shapes or Shapes Requested by Child
Paper Strip. 1" x 2" (body)
(Child's name on back.)

Procedure

1. Small group discussion.
a. Talk about butterflies; have pictures and models.
b. Talk about and demonstrate the steps of making a Butterfly.
c. Ask who would like to make something like a Butterfly.
d. Encourage children to tell you other things that could be made in this way.
e. Talk about and demonstrate tearing tissue paper.
f. Pass out tissue paper to be torn.

2. Child tears tissue paper strips into pieces. (Some children may lose interest after tearing and move to another activity.)
3. Talk about and demonstrate gluing on waxed paper.
4. Teacher sets up child's work area for gluing.
5. Child glues body strip in the middle of the Butterfly shape.
6. Child glues torn tissue paper pieces onto the shape he has chosen.
7. Talk about and demonstrate safety rules for hot irons.
Note: Make up and follow class rules for safe use of hot irons.
8. Teacher seals child's project.
a. Lay down several sheets of newsprint.
b. On top of the newsprint place the waxed paper shape with the tissue paper glued on it.
c. Place string beside the 1" x 2" body strip.
d. On top of that place the second waxed paper shape (matching the 2 shapes).
e. On top of the two matched shapes, place several sheets of newsprint.
f. Iron the top sheet of newsprint. The heat will warm the waxed paper enough to melt the wax, binding the shapes together.
9. Child helps to clean up work area.

13

Children's Ideas

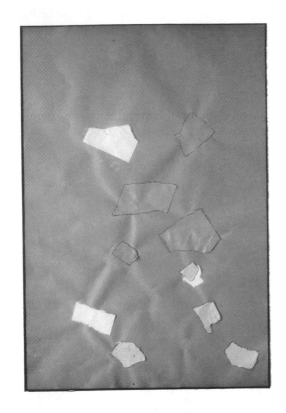

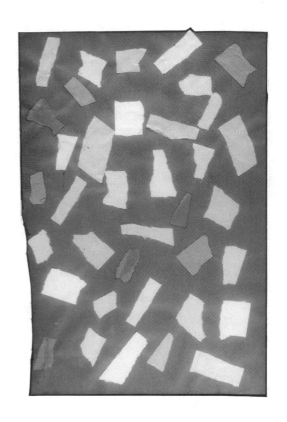

Children's Ideas

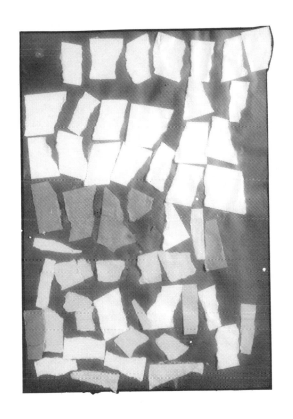

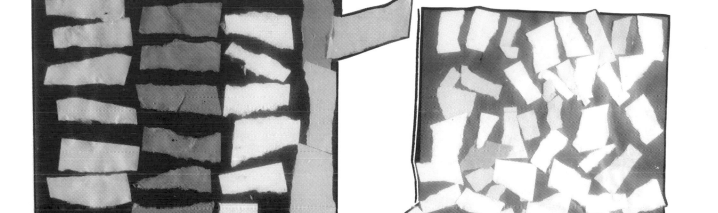

Teacher Ideas

1. Make tools and materials available for children to use independently. **You decide for your classroom how much adult supervision is required.**
2. Use other pre-cut forms: kites, animals, flowers, etc.
3. Make waxed paper balloons, clouds, a fish in a bowl, a collage.
4. Use nursery rhymes and finger plays for pre-cut form ideas.
5. Make a Headband for each holiday.
6. See Skill One Snip.
7. Make other non-toxic items available to tear (e.g., leaves, old material, lettuce, playdough, etc).

Bilateral
Tearing Motion

I. Instructions
A. Skill
1. One hand pulls away from the body.
2. Second hand pulls toward the body.

Note: Given ample opportunity to tear most children will develop this skill naturally.

B. Language

				17
tearing	opposite	ripping	long	
short	away from	toward body	grain	

C. Short Tear

Note: Paper has a direction or grain. It tears more smoothly with the grain.

1. Materials: Newspaper strips, 6" high and as long as the width of one page.
2. Procedure
   a. Fingers grab top edge of the length of the strip.
   b. One hand moves out and away from the body. Second hand moves in and toward the body.
   c. Paper tears top to bottom across the 6" height.

D. Long Tear

1. Materials: Newspaper strips, 12" wide x the width of one page.
2. Procedure
   a. Hands and fingers as in short tear.
   b. Paper tears top to bottom down 12" length.

II. Problems and Solutions
A. Child pulls paper as in Skill One.
1. Return to Skill One (accept child's present level).
2. Use classroom activities for hand strength and coordination.
3. Continue to give the child tearing opportunities with narrow strips.

B. Irregular Tear
1. Paper has a direction or grain; it tears irregularly one way and smoothly the other. Hand the paper to the child in such a way that he will tear with the grain, which is the direction to get a smooth tear.
2. See Skill One Reciprocal Tearing Motion.

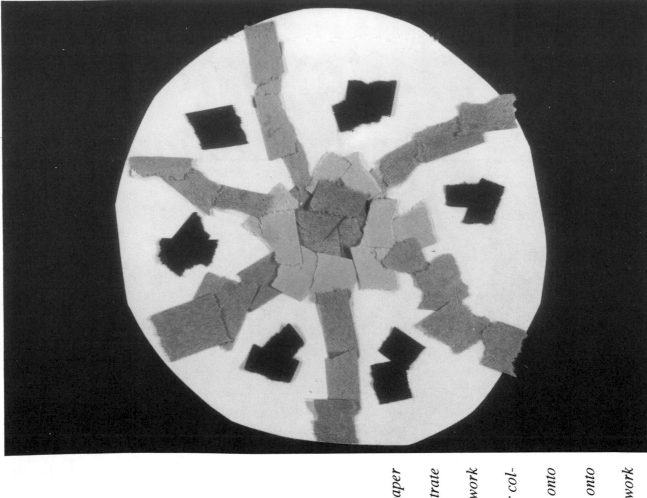

Collage

Supplies

Glue
Paper Towels
Scrap Box

Teacher-Prepared Materials

Paper Strips, 1" x 12"
Paper Circle, 6" diameter
Other Irregular Shapes
Background Paper, 9" x 12"
(Child's name on back.)

Procedure

1. Small group discussion.
a. Talk about collages; show sample designs.
b. Talk about and demonstrate bilateral tearing.
c. Ask: "Who would like to tear paper?" (Some children may only tear the paper and be finished, with no interest in gluing.)
d. Talk about and demonstrate how to make a collage.
e. Pass out 1" x 12" paper strips.

2. Child tears 1" x 12" paper strips into pieces.

3. Talk about and demonstrate using the glue.

4. Teacher sets up child's work area for gluing.

5. Child chooses shape for collage base.

6. Child glues torn pieces onto base shape.

7. Child glues paper shape onto background paper.

8. Child helps to clean up work area.

Can Collage

Supplies

Scissors
Glue
Paper Towels
Can - Covered with construction paper
(Child's name on bottom.)
Scrap Box

Teacher-Prepared Materials

3 Paper Strips, 1" x 12"
Paper Strip long enough to wrap around
outside of can.

Procedure

1. *Small group discussion.*
   a. Talk about decorating a can.
   b. Ask who would like to decorate a can. (Some children may only want to draw on the can; others may choose not to make a can.)
   c. Let the children tell you how to tear the strips.
   d. Pass out strips to be torn.

2. *Child tears the 1" x 12" into pieces of varied lengths.*

3. *Child may choose items from the scrap box.*

4. *Let the children tell you about how to use the glue.*

5. *Let children select color of can cover; pass out cans.*

6. *Child plans design for covered can.*

7. *Set up for gluing; help child understand he must hold piece in place until it dries.*

8. *Clean up.*

19

Bear

Supplies

Glue
Paper Towels
Scrap Box

Teacher-Prepared Materials

6 Paper Strips, 1" x 12" (fur)
Pre-cut Eyes, Nose, Mouth
Pre-cut Bear Shape, and Other Shapes (Animals and odd shapes.) (Child's name on back.)

Procedure

1. Small group discussion.
a. Talk about bears; read a bear story; have and show pictures of bears.
b. Talk about and demonstrate bilateral tearing.
c. Talk about and demonstrate how to make a Bear or the shape they have chosen.
d. Let the children tell you about:

  1. their experiences with Bears;
  2. bilateral tearing;
  3. how to make their Bears or the shapes they have chosen;
  4. if they would like to make an animal or just tear.

e. Let children choose background shapes.
f. Pass out 1" x 12" paper strips.

2. Child tears 1" x 12" paper strips into fur. (Some children may just want to tear paper, then move on to another activity.)

3. Talk about and demonstrate using glue.

4. Teacher sets up child's work area for gluing.

5. Child glues:
  a. fur to bear shape, or to the shape he has chosen;
  b. eyes, nose, mouth to bear shape or other chosen shape;
  c. pieces he has chosen from the Scrap Box.

6. Child helps to clean up work area.

WADE PARK SCHOOL

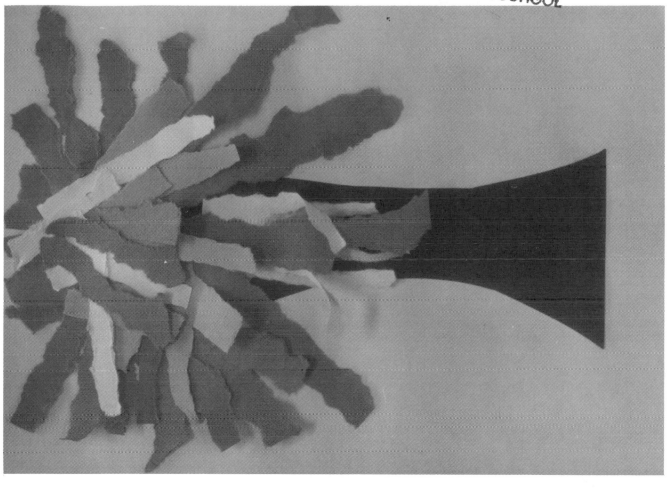

Tree

Supplies

Glue
Paper Towels
Scrap Box

Teacher-Prepared Materials

4 Paper Rectangles, 6" x 12" (Limbs and Leaves)
Cut paper so that tearing with the grain produces 6" strips.
Pre-cut Tree Trunk
Background Paper, 9" x 12" (Child's name on back.)

Procedure

1. Small group discussion.
a. Talk about trees; show pictures.
b. Talk about and demonstrate bilateral tearing.
c. Talk about and demonstrate how to make a Tree.
d. Let children tell you about:
 1. bilateral tearing;
 2. how to make their Trees;
 3. other things they can make with this paper;
 4. what they want to make.
e. Pass out 6" x 12" paper rectangles.

2. Child tears 6" x 12" rectangles into 6" strips for limbs and leaves. (Some children will only be interested in tearing.)

3. Talk about and demonstrate using glue.

4. Teacher sets up child's work area for gluing.

5. Child glues:
 a. tree trunk to background paper;
 b. leaves and limbs to tree trunk;
 c. pieces as he likes to make his own creation.

6. Child helps to clean up work area.

Long Tear Mobile

Supplies

Glue
Paper Towels
String 16" long tied to
Cardboard strip 2" x 18"
Scrap Box

Teacher-Prepared Materials

4 Paper rectangles 9" x 12"
(cut paper so that tearing with the grain produces 9" strips.)

Procedure

1. Small group discussion.
a. Talk about mobiles, have some hanging in your classroom.
b. Talk about a long bilateral tear.
c. Talk about how the children could make their mobiles.
d. Let children tell you about:
 1. making a long tear;
 2. what they will do with their long tears.
e. Pass out 9" x 12" rectangles.
2. Child tear 9" x 12" rectangles into 9" strips.

3. For some children this will be the entire activity.
4. Talk about:
a. gluing the strips onto the 2" x 18" cardboard strip;
b. waiting for the glue to dry.
5. Teacher sets up work area for gluing.
6. Child selects items from the scrap box.

7. Child glues:
a. torn paper strip onto cardboard strip in a way that pleases her;
b. items from the scrap box onto her creation;
c. her torn pieces, scrap box items and cardboard strip in a way that pleases her.

8. *Child helps to clean up.*
9. *Talk with children about ways to display their creations.*
10. *Some may want to keep it and walk around with it.*

Note: Some of your children may only want to tear strips. They may want to save them or throw them away. Let your children be creative with their design.

Paper Bag Puppet

Supplies

Glue
Paper Towels
Small Paper Bag
Scrap Box

Teacher-Prepared Materials

Paper Rectangle, 9" x 12" (Hair)
Cut Paper (so that tearing with the grain produces 9" strips.)
2 Paper Strips, 1" x 12" (Design)
Pre-cut Eyes, Nose, Mouth, Ears

Procedure

1. Small group discussion.
   a. Talk about puppets; have hand puppets from your room.
   b. Talk about a long tear and a short tear.
   c. Talk about and demonstrate how to make a Puppet.
   d. Let child tell you about:
      1. long and short tears;
      2. how to make her Puppet;
      3. what she would like to do with her paper bag.

   e. Pass out 9" x 12" rectangles and 1" x 9" x 12" into 9" strips.
2. Child tears:
   a. 9" x 12" into 9" for hair;
   b. 1" x 12" into pieces for design;
   c. other pieces in a way that pleases her.

3. Talk about and demonstrate:
   a. using glue;
   b. gluing mouth;
      1. upper lip on bag bottom;
      2. lower lip on bag side next to bottom;
      3. thus child can open and close the Puppet's mouth.
4. Teacher sets up child's work area for gluing.

5. Child glues:
   a. mouth to bag as in 3;
   b. eyes and nose to bottom of bag;
   c. ears to side of bag;
   d. hair to bottom of bag;
   e. design to side of bag.
6. Child makes a Puppet of her own design.
7. Child helps to clean up.

Note: Making and using this puppet helps to develop the opening strength for hands needed for scissoring.

23

Children's Ideas

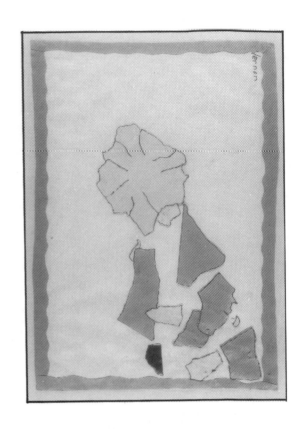

"I made a butterfly"

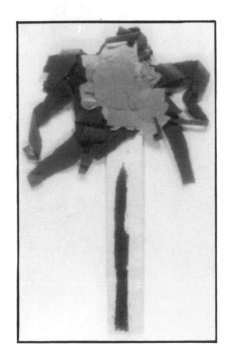

Teacher Ideas

1. Make newsprint and other scrap paper available for children to tear for fun.
2. See Reciprocal Tearing.
3. See Skill One Snip.
4. Make a door size display for class projects.
5. Tear something non-toxic other than paper just for the fun of tearing (e.g., lettuce, cloth, leaves, playdough, etc.)
6. See chart for activities to develop pre-scissoring hand coordination. Make appropriate materials available for children to use independently.

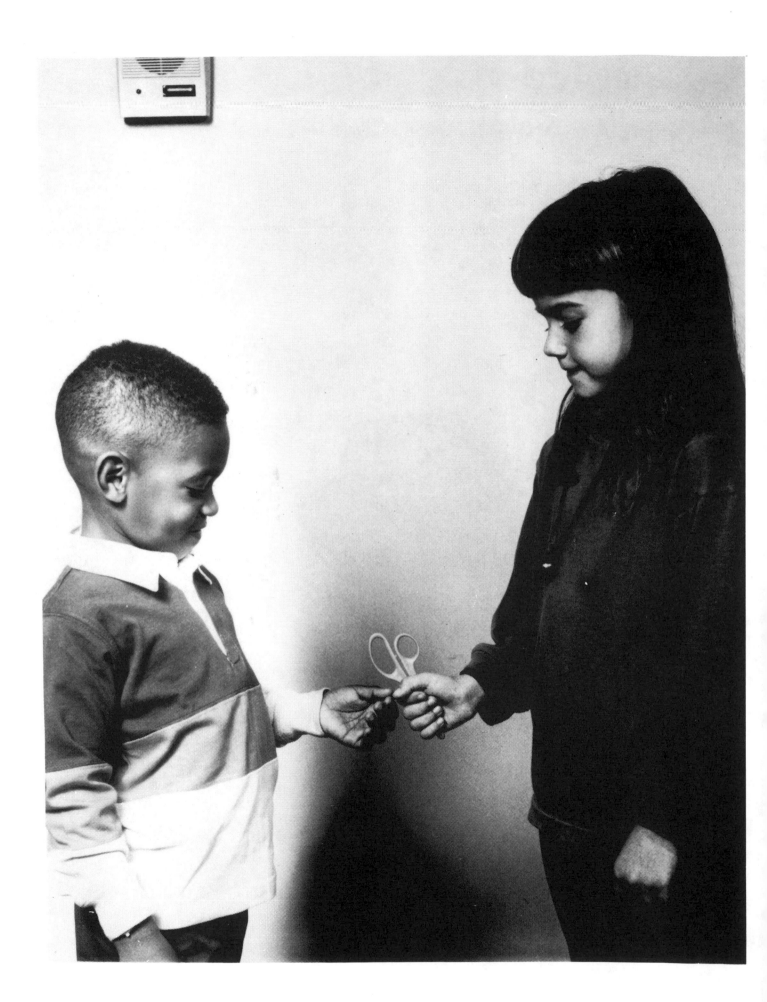

Chapter Three
Scissors,
Paper,
Clean - Up

When children are learning the art of cutting, the quality of their cutting tool plays an important role. Scissors designed to be cute or scissors of poor quality present unnecessary frustrations to children learning to cut. Children deserve high-quality scissors and the success these tools bring to learning the art. Quality scissors are made of forged steel and have an adjustment screw, and may have rubber-coated handles. Premium Scissors have a brand name, Fiskars®. The care and research put into the development of these scissors are well worth their price. By comparison shopping, you can reduce the price of Fiskars® considerably. So shop around.

Plastic scissors with reinforced metal blades will cut some paper. Plastic scissors allow a child with undeveloped muscle strength to cut more easily. The flexibility of the plastic material allows a right or left-handed child to use the right-handed scissors. Plastic scissors do not cut well for very long.

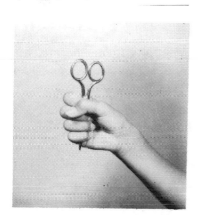

Provide 5-inch, bluntnose scissors for the initial cutting

experiences. Have available right- or left-handed scissors to meet the needs of the child's handedness. Fiskars® are so well tooled that left-handed children can find success with this right-handed tool during the free cutting sequence; because of the placement of the line, this same child may require left-handed scissors for the line cutting sequence.

As children gain control of the tool, they may move to 5-inch, clip-point scissors. Check frequently for the sharpness of the blades and the tightness or looseness of the screw. The ease with which the scissors cut makes a great difference in the children's success with their cutting activities.

Safety should be an initial concern when teaching the use of scissors, and should be thoroughly discussed immediately. Make up "Do Rules" to let your children know what they can do with their scissors. (Do stay at the table. Do return them to the scissors container. Do hand them to another child safely, etc.) Children must be taught how to hold the scissors when walking with them or handing

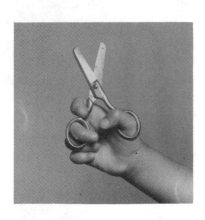

them to someone else. The hand makes a fist around the scissors' blades. The pointed end sticks out of the fist towards the floor just enough so as not to jab the body and not so far in as to jab the hand if he should fall. Children should also learn to be aware of where their scissors are in relation to their bodies. Incidental waving or pointing should be considered a misuse of the scissors.

Children need to realize the dangers involved when using scissors and have a respect for the proper use of the tool. When these concepts are understood by a child, his self-concept becomes more positive in two ways. First, knowing he is trusted to use the tool properly will give him a "grown-up" feeling. Second, the doors to self expression are opened wider by his using a "grownup" creative tool safely.

Finger placement is important. When using Fiskars®, the pointer finger goes in front of the large loop. The remaining 2 or 3 fingers go into the loop, depending on the size of the child's hand. The thumb goes into the second loop. For standard metal scissors the loops are designed to fit around the thumb and middle finger. (Thumb in one hole, trigger/ pointer/index finger in front of the second hole.) This placement is the same for right-handed and left-handed children. The position of the loop of the middle joint on the middle finger will vary with each child and each cutting task. Although some children may

begin cutting with the loop on the first or last joint if the cutting task is not too difficult for them, they will move the loop to a comfortable position on the middle joint naturally . Physically small children may prefer to place more than one finger in the loop. They should still begin with the second finger, so that the index finger remains in its position in front of the loop. Children who are relearning to hold scissors may "float" the index finger at first.

However, as these children work through planned cutting experiences at the children's developmental level, the "floating finger" will learn its position and help to guide and balance the scissors. There are two reasons why the finger placement described above is the most efficient way to hold the scissors: 1. Tool balance; 2. Hand strength (the second finger is stronger than the index finger.)

Author's comment: For those of you who are saying "But I don't hold scissors that way", neither did I. Cut "that way" for one month. You will wonder how you ever managed to cut any other way. Had I not been willing to try "that way," this book may never have been written.

During initial cutting experiences, the scissor hand's major movement should be an open/ close motion. The other hand holds the paper, moving it slowly into an easy cutting position.

When children are given scissors at the appropriate develop-

velopmental level and are presented with an appropriate cutting task, they will assume a natural, relaxed sitting or standing position: the elbow is bent, and the hands and forearms are almost perpendicular to the body. Physically normal children can easily maintain this relaxed position while cutting. The child who contorts his body and tenses his muscles while cutting needs either to return to a simpler task and/or return to the related activities that develop the necessary skills for learning to cut. He should not be required or allowed to cut in such opposition to his body. Help him to relax his body during cutting.

We are becoming more aware of the child with special needs: he may have a specific learning disability, be emotionally and/or mentally handicapped. Teachers of these children are aware of the children's sporadic developmental patterns. They may be able to accomplish the activities related to cutting but still be unable to cut. To help these children, there are double-looped scissors. These allow a child to hold the scissors while an adult helper's hand holds the child's hand and the scissors. These scissors have proven to be very helpful in aiding the learning process of both normal and handicapped children. *Note: Teachers and/or parents of normal children who may see this aid as a way to teaching their child to cut "early." Believe in your child's eagerness to learn. If he has trouble, allow him*

time to develop neurologically, muscularly, and mentally to the point where he can succeed alone. Please do not use double-looped scissors to force him to learn because you are ready to teach him.

Ample paper should be provided for young children learning to cut. Scrap paper surrounds us daily and is thrown away. Get your friends to rescue it for your children. Your local printer is a good source. Ask your parents if printing is done where they work. Printers will have long strips which will be perfect for all the headbands your children will be making.

For beginning snipping, a paper that will not bend over the blades is the most desirable kind of paper. After snipping, the most available paper is newspaper, magazine pages, greeting cards and computer readouts. Construction paper has a good stiffness. A thick paper increases the difficulty of the task. By using "scraps" you can allow the children to cut for as long as they desire at each skill level. This practice cutting can be the "purpose" of the activity. When they finish this practice session with scrap paper, the children can feel free to throw all of their cuttings into the trash can. Thus, a child has used some of our scrap to learn something before the scrap goes to the sanitary land fill. Remember to place more value on the new skills the child is learning than on one piece of paper.

This is not to say that chil-

29

dren should be allowed to be wasteful. Teach them that some paper comes from a very valuable resource — our trees — giving them another experience in natural resource conservation. Talk about your community's effort to recycle its used paper. Also talk with the children about sizes so that they will select amounts of paper in a quantity proportionate to their project. Help them realize they can use scrap and do not need a whole new sheet of paper for each piece they wish to cut out.

As the skill of the children increases, many kinds of paper, cloth, and other materials should be provided. Scissors appropriate for cutting these materials should be made available to the children.

Because you have already taught the child about organizing the work area, the child will want to know where to put the scissors. An easy placement is on the work surface in front of the child and the work area. This should be "scissors' place" and no other materials should be put there. This "scissors' place," avoids the problems of the scissors being lost under the scraps, knocked off the edge of the table, and/or being thrown away with the scraps.

Clean-up should be considered a part of the cutting experience. Children should be required to clean up after themselves. Picking up the scraps will help children to be aware of where scraps fall during cutting. Scissors should always be cleaned and dried before being put away. About every three months, have a scissors cleaning time with adult supervision. Wash them with soap and dry them; then put a drop of sewing machine oil at the screw joint to insure a smoother and longer cutting life. Also, cut a fine grade of folded sandpaper. This will help to sharpen the blades of forged steel scissors. Allowing the children to care for their tools will help them have respect for the scissors.

Teach the children to think about a safe place to store their scissors:

1. where an inexperienced child cannot get them easily;

2. so the points do not jab them when they reach for the scissors the next time they want to use scissors;

3. in a container with points down, out of which the scissors will not fall easily if it is dropped;

4. where the scissors will remain clean and dry, ready for use again.

Basic patterns for tool quality and design, safety, respect for the tool, finger placement, cutting posture, paper supply, organization of work area, cleanup and care of scissors have been explained in this chapter, to help each cutting experience be successful. The patterns are designed to allow the children to develop a responsible attitude toward their role in learning.

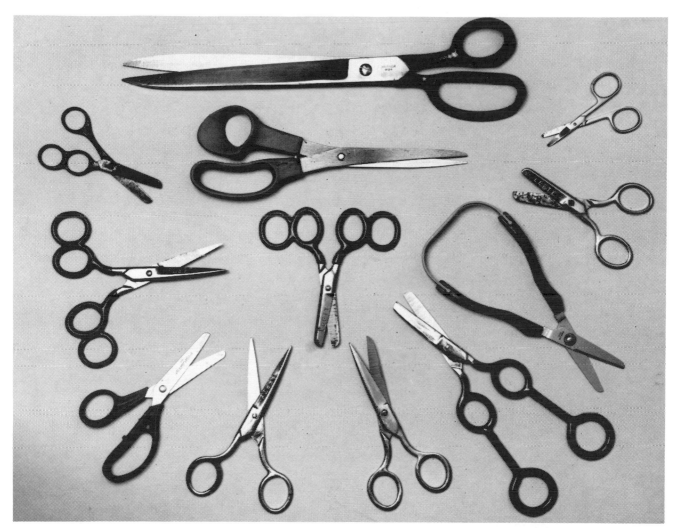

Kinds of scissors, left to right: right-handed 3" beginner two looped; left-handed 7" sharp double-looped teacher training; right-handed 5" blunt Fiskars®; left-handed 5" sharp; right-handed 5" clip point; right-handed 5" blunt double-looped teacher training; right-handed 3" blunt easy grip; left-handed 5" blunt; right-handed 2" baby nail; top to bottom: right-handed 18" teacher/office shears; right-handed 12" dressmaker shears; left-handed 5" blunt teacher training.

Teacher Ideas

1. Find a source for scrap paper:
   a. call local printer;
   b. talk to parents about the paper which is thrown away at their work place
2. Make paper available for children to cut.
3. You decide how available scissors will be in your classroom. Some children need continual supervison while scissors are available.
4. For physically small children, use baby scissors. (Sold to cut baby's fingernails, these have a blunt end.)

Chapter Four

Free Cutting Sequence

Often, along with mastery of a skill comes the attitude that the skill is easily acquired, when indeed the many steps leading toward mastery were a gradual and complicated process. So it is with cutting.

As adults, we should appreciate the feelings a child brings to the learning situation, and be willing to provide an environment designed to allow the child to master new skills at his own rate. This cutting sequence attempts to require the child to develop only one step at a time and to meet with success at each level, thus allowing a gradual flow of individual steps to develop naturally into the mastery of the skill of cutting. This process allows the child to master the skill through a series of positive successful experiences. Thus, his self-concept is enhanced at each skill level.

Throughout this chapter, the format will be as follows:

1. A new skill will be introduced. Instruction will be given to the teacher for presentation to the child and observation of

skill development. Instructions for the left-handed child mirror those for the right-handed child.

2. Problems which may arise are listed and some solutions are given. Reference is made as to which developmental task from Chapter 1 should be provided to enhance developmental growth when required.

3. Activities are structured so that the children will become used to an organizational pattern for doing these activities. The organized child will then be able to use his energies on creativity within each activity, as he develops expressive language and visual perceptions of his world. The project directions are for the teacher's comfort level. Please note that the structure serves to give the child a sense of order to her work, NOT to dictate how each piece should be placed on the project. Helping the child to order her world allows her the freedom to express her creativity on each project. Remember, after you give the child the paper pieces they belong to her. She should decide how she wants to place

them on her paper. Believe in her development and help her be proud of her present skill level.

Always have extra pre-cut pieces as well as your scrap box available for your children. This encourages them to make their own decisions about how their project should look.

Note: Each child should be given the option of not choosing any particular "project." She should be able to create her own ideas or move on to another activity in the classroom. <u>Do</u> *continue to encourage children to tear paper for* **34** *their projects. They need the experience for pre-writing development.*

The child should be encouraged to use the activities as a guide to his own creations. The child should be instructed not to copy the model exactly. Hopefully, he will add what pleases him to each activity or perhaps invent his own project with the materials you have given him.

Author's comment: When working with the children I do not use a sample or an art model if we are making realistic items. I have available a model or pictures of that item (e.g., horse, flowers, the children themselves, ball, etc.) We spend a lot of time talking about what we could make, then talk specifically about each piece of pre-cut paper and which part of the end product it could be (e.g., body, legs, tree trunk). By allowing the children to construct these pieces in their

"mind's eye," they will find four or five ways to put together whatever they are making. Most of the activities in this book are a result of child planning. So encourage your children to use their own plan. You and they will be delighted with how creative and inventive their projects will be.

When you and the children are developing your own activities, remember all the songs and poems you use with your children. They love to have something to recite about their products. As you move along through the skills you will understand better what to expect from your children and you will find creating your own activities is fun and rewarding. Also give the children daily opportunities with an odd assortment of pre-cut paper and see what they create. They will love cutting this paper. Please don't worry about how much they cut and throw away. Because you have found a source of scrap paper, your children will have plenty of paper to expend on their creative instincts.

There are two tools which will save you time and energy in preparing the pre-cut paper for your children. A paper cutter and a pair of office/teacher's scissors are essential. Be sure these are of high quality. Teachers as well as children deserve high quality scissors.

As was said earlier, discussion of the words relating to cutting is also important for the children. Expand their understanding of language through

the experience of cutting. Encourage the children to use the language presented at each skill level, as well as the language needed to describe each project.

Initially, as well as with each new step, cutting is freehand (e.g., no lines to follow). Close observation of a child learning to cut reveals that cutting on a line complicates the task at hand. This is more obvious when thinking in terms of learning to ride a tricycle and/or bicycle. You would not require the child to follow a line in his initial experiences of learning to ride. Or, at a fine motor level, consider the initial use of crayon and/or pencils and the need for much "free hand" use of the tool before lines are introduced. This cutting sequence is based on child-tested research. Children have shown us that the best way to teach them scissoring skills is without lines to worry them. As your children learn this sequence, teach it to yourself. You will be amazed at what you can "free cut."

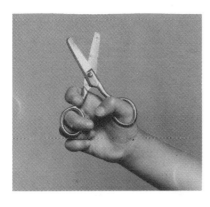

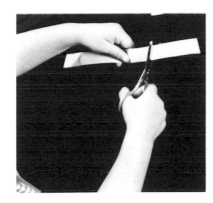

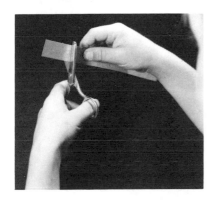

Skill One

Snip

I. Instructions

A. Skill

Scissor Manipulation

B. Language

scissors	scissors blade	screw	loop
hand	finger	joint	first
second	thumb	right	left
out	open	close	hold
all the way	in front	start	snip
narrow	guide		

C. Materials

Paper Strips: Length does not matter
Width - 2/3's the length of the scissor blade

D. Procedure

1. See Chapter II for "Cutting Posture."
   This relaxed posture does contribute to the ease with which the child cuts.
2. Cutting begins at the end of the paper nearest the scissors hand.
3. One snip is required to cut off a piece of the paper strip.
4. Scissors close.

II. Problems and Solutions

A. Difficulty in opening and closing the scissors.

1. Check scissors for correct handedness.
2. Check size of the scissors for the hand.
3. Check scissors for cleanliness
4. Check tightness of the screw joint.
5. Provide the prehension activities that develop the hand muscles, gross and fine motor movement.
6. Allow time for practice in opening and closing the scissors.

B. Paper folding as the child tries to cut.

1. Paper should be held at a 90° angle to the scissors.
2. Paper should remain at a 90° angle to the scissors when laid across the blade. If it bends over, it is too lightweight.
3. Use card weight paper.
4. Joint screw may be too loose.
5. Check scissors for correct handedness.

C. Paper tearing as the child tries to cut.

1. Coordination of the hands; provide use of hands activities: i.e., tearing paper, bead stringing, finger play.
2. Joint screw may be too tight.
3. Paper may be too lightweight (too thin.)

D. An incomplete cut although the child closes the scissors completely.

1. The task is too difficult for the developmental level of the child.
   a. Return to Bilateral Integration; Use of Hands; and Prehension Activities.
   b. Some success may be achieved if you hold the paper on either side of the scissors, allowing the child to concentrate only on the cutting motion of the hand.

E. Perseveration - Cutting air; i.e., the child gets stuck on opening and closing the scissors rather than beginning and/or completing the cutting activity.

1. First, allow that the child may be delighted with himself that he can manipulate the scissors. If, after several experiences with scissors, he continues to "cut air"
   a. look for inability to stop other actions, such as running, painting, eating (motor functions);
   b. watch to see if it is the sound that is pleasing rather than an inability to stop a motion (auditory function).
2. In either case, reduce as much as possible the distractions to the child during the cutting ...even to sitting him by himself at the beginning of the activity. Explain that he is not being punished; rather, he is sitting alone to help him cut better.
3. Again, in either case a change in mode of activity may help. Have the child cut, put down the scissors, put cut paper in the container, return to cutting and repeat the pattern. This way he may not get stuck on the cutting action. Gradually increase the number of cuts he may do in one pattern.
4. If his problem is an auditory function, then a positive repetitive verbal reminder ("cut the paper") may interrupt his perseveration, allowing him to "shift gears" and continue with his cutting activity.
5. For motor function problems:
   a. See Skill Two Problems A, 1 and 2 for cutting.
   b. Tearing Paper
      1. First setting up a pattern as in #3, have the child: tear, put torn paper in a container, tear and repeat the pattern.
      2. Have the child stop tearing the paper on cue.
   c. As in 4, a positive repetitive verbal cue may be used.

Collage

Supplies

Scissors
Glue
Paper Towels
Scrap Box

Teacher-Prepared Materials

8 Paper Strips, 2/3 the length of the scissors blade x 12" long
Background Paper, 9" x 12' (Child's name on the back.)

Procedure

1. Small group discussion.
   a. Talk about and demonstrate using scissors to snip and how to hold the scissors.
   b. Talk about a collage and how to make one.
   c. Pass out scissors and Teacher-Prepared Materials.
2. Child snips paper strips into pieces. (Snipping may be the complete activity for some children. They may want to save their cuttings or just throw them away.)
3. Teacher sets up work area for gluing. (Gluing may be a separate activity.)
4. Children talk about gluing.
5. Child glues cut paper pieces onto his 9" x 12" background paper, in a design that pleases the child.
6. Child helps to clean up work area.

Fish

Supplies

Scissors
Glue
Paper Towels
Scrap Box

Teacher-Prepared Materials

6 Paper Strips 2/3 the length of the scissors blade x 12" long (Fish Scales)
Paper Fish Shape and Other Shapes
(Child's name on back.)

Procedure

1. *Small group discussion.*
a. *Talk about fish; have pictures/models.*
b. *Talk about how to make a fish.*
c. *Ask children what other shapes they would like to have.*
d. *Pass out paper to be cut.*
2. *Child snips print strips into pieces.*
3. *Teacher sets up child's work area for gluing.*
4. *Child glues his cut pieces onto chosen paper shape.*
5. *Child helps to clean up work area.*

Note: Some of your children may only want to snip with their scissors. They may want to save their cuttings or just throw them away.

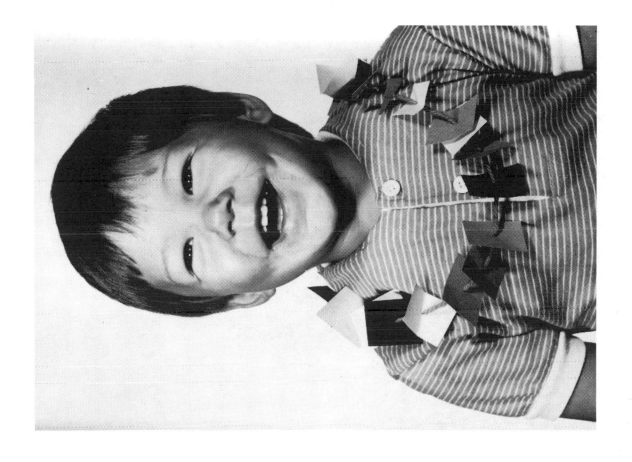

Necklace

Supplies

Scissors
Yarn/String 36"
Blunt Tapestry Needles
Scrap Box

Teacher-Prepared Materials

Paper Strips 2/3 the length of the scissors blade x 12" long
Threaded Needle

Procedure

1. *Small group discussion.*
   a. Talk about using scissors to snip and the safety rules for using scissors.
   b. Talk about how to make a Necklace.
   c. Pass out scissors and Teacher-Prepared Materials, except for string and yarn.
2. *Child cuts paper strips into pieces.*
3. *Teacher writes child's name on one of the snipped paper pieces.*
4. *Children talk about and demonstrate safety rules for using needles. (This could be an activity for a second day).*

5. *Pass out threaded needles.* **Note: Do not leave any child unsupervised with a needle. If the adult needs to leave the group, ALL needles should be taken from the children.**

6. *Teacher supervises child stringing cut paper pieces onto yarn.*

7. *The child may choose to string some of the pieces from the scrap box.*

8. *Teacher ties the ends of the yarn together.*

9. *Child helps to clean up work area.*

Note: Using the scissors may be a complete activity in itself for some children.

Headband

Supplies

Scissors
Glue
Paper Towels
Scrap Box

Teacher-Prepared Materials

8 Paper Strips 2/3 the length of the scissors blade x 12" long
Paper Strip 6" x 24" (Child's name on back.)

Procedure

1. Small group discussion.

a. Talk again about the safety rules for using scissors.

b. Talk about and demonstrate the steps in making a headband.

c. Ask the children: "Who would like to make a headband?"

d. Pass out scissors and Teacher-Prepared Materials.

2. Child snips the paper strips into pieces.

3. Child may find additional things in the Scrap Box.

4. Talk about and demonstrate rules for using glue.

5. Teacher sets up child's work area for glue.

6. Child glues pieces from the scrap box and the cut paper pieces onto the 6" x 24" paper strip.

7. Child helps to clean up work area.

8. Teacher fits Headband to child's head and staples ends together.

Seasonal Tree Collage

Supplies

Scissors
Glue
Paper Towels
Pencils/Crayons/Markers
Scrap Box

Teacher-Prepared Materials

Paper Strips, 2/3 the length of the scissors blade x 12" long, in a variety of fall leaf colors; flower colors; summer leaf colors; snow.
Paper Trees (trunk and limbs)
Background Paper 9" x 12"
(Child's name on the back.)

Procedure

1. *Small group discussion.*
   a. Talk about seasons and trees; have pictures and models.
   b. Talk about and demonstrate how to make a Seasonal Tree Collage.
   c. Talk about cutting posture.
   d. Pass out scissors and Teacher-Prepared Materials.
   e. Let children tell you about the trees at school, at home or anywhere in the child's experience.
   f. Let children tell you what each piece of paper could become.
   g. Let children tell you what they will make with their pieces of paper.
2. *Child snips the paper strips into leaves/flowers/snow.*
3. *Child lays out cut pieces on the background paper in a way that pleases the child.*
4. *Child may add items from scrap box.*
5. *Teacher sets up child's work area for gluing.*
6. *Child glues:*
   a. the trunk and limb pieces;
   b. the leaves/flowers/snow onto the trees, in the sky and onto the ground;
   c. the extra pieces where it pleases him.
7. *Child helps to clean up work area (except for pencils/crayons/markers).*
8. *After glue has dried, child adds drawing to the Seasonal Tree Collage (or to his own project).*

Note: Cutting and gluing may be treated as two separate activities.

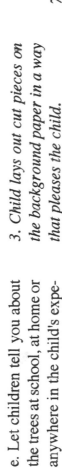

41

Class Mural

Supplies

Scissors
Glue
Paper Towels

Teacher-Prepared Materials

8 Paper Strips 2/3 the length of the scissor blade x 12" long.
Butcher Paper 3' x 6"
Background Paper 8 1/2" x 11" (Child's name on back.)

Procedure

1. *Class discussion.*
   a. Talk about murals; identify any your children have seen.
   b. Ask children where the mural could go in their classroom.
   c. Let children tell you about safe use of scissors.
   d. Pass out scissors and Teacher-Prepared Materials.
2. *Child snips the paper strips into pieces.*
3. *This will be the end of the activity for some children.*
4. *Talk about each child's space on the mural.*
   a. ask who would like to glue their pieces onto the mural;
   b. select a small group and identify each child's space on the mural.
5. *Remaining children:*
   a. set up work area for gluing;
   b. work together gluing pieces on the mural;
   c. some children may want to glue cut pieces onto 8 1/2" x 11" background sheet.
6. *Some children may offer words to go along with their cuttings.*
7. *Child helps to clean up the work area.*
8. *This mural is easily an on-going project that some children will want to glue their cuttings onto. Display it at eye level for continued interaction.*

Note: Children may create independent ideas with these materials.

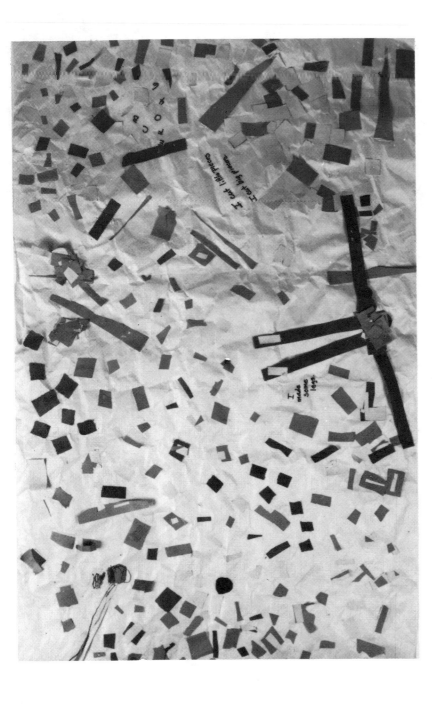

42

Children's Ideas

Children's Ideas

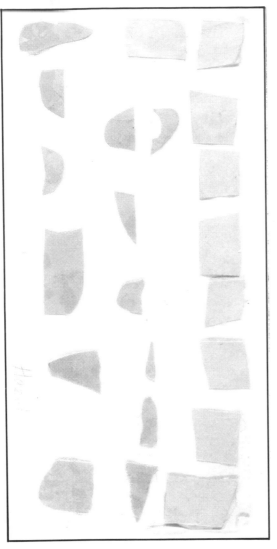

Teacher Ideas

1. Make paper and scissors available to children for the joy of cutting. Even allow them to cut over the trash can with no concern for the paper after it has fallen in the trash can.
2. Provide envelopes for them to keep their cuttings in, to save and take home.
3. See tearing activities for additional ideas.
4. Use old scissors to cut play dough or dried leaves.

Skill Two
Fringe

I. Instructions

A. Skill
Stopping the scissoring action.

B. Language
fringe   do not close   stop

C. Materials
Paper Strips - Length 6" - Width about one inch longer than the scissors blade.

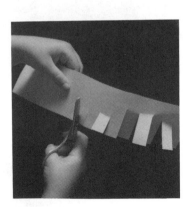

D. Procedure
1. Relaxed "cutting posture."
2. Cutting begins at the end of the paper nearest the scissors hand.
3. Scissors blades are completely opened.
4. One cut across the width of the paper.
5. At the point where the paper-holding hand needs to move, the scissors blades should hold the paper.
6. Scissors DO NOT close. (This is an essential skill.)

II. Problems and Solutions

A. The child may find it difficult to stop the scissor action or not to close the scissors completely. The problem here may be a lack of development of motor control.

1. Can he stop a gross motor function? When walking, can he stop on cue, or does it take him a few steps to stop? Any of the bilateral integration or gross motor development activities that lend themselves to freezing will help him develop the ability to stop a gross motor action.
2. Check stopping a fine motor action. Develop this skill by using the activities for fine motor development that lend themselves to freezing (e.g., playdough, tracing, painting, tearing,etc.)
3. Now back to the scissors. Put a piece of masking tape across the width of the strip where the child is to stop cutting. This will provide visual and kinesthetic clues for stopping the scissors. After the child has had much success with the tape guide, a magic marker line down the length of the strip can provide a stopping guide until the child can cue himself on stopping the action of the scissors.
4. In addition or by itself, a verbal cue of "stop" may be helpful, particularly if the child is an auditory learner.
5. See Skill One, E. Perseveration.

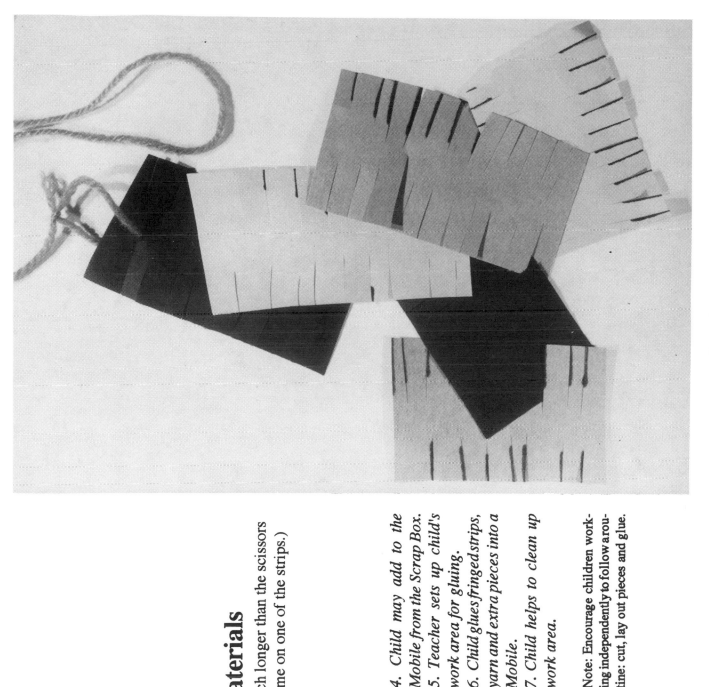

Mobile

Supplies

Scissors
Glue
Paper Towels
String/Yarn 16" long
Scrap Box

Teacher-Prepared Materials

6 Paper Strips: width at least one inch longer than the scissors blade; length 3" to 6". (Child's name on one of the strips.)

Procedure

1. Small group discussion.
a. Talk about mobiles; ask children where they have seen them; have models.
b. Talk about and demonstrate how to fringe.
c. Pass out scissors and Teacher-Prepared Materials.
2. Child fringes the paper strips (Fringing may be a complete activity for some children.)
3. Child plans how the fringed strips will be laid out.

4. Child may add to the Mobile from the Scrap Box.
5. Teacher sets up child's work area for gluing.
6. Child glues fringed strips, yarn and extra pieces into a Mobile.
7. Child helps to clean up work area.

Note: Encourage children working independently to follow a routine: cut, lay out pieces and glue.

Fringed Headband

Supplies

Scissors
Glue
Paper Towels
Stapler
Scrap Box

Teacher-Prepared Materials

Paper Circles, 6" diameter
Paper Circles, 3" diameter
Paper Strip 6" x 24" (Child's name on the back.)

Procedure

1. Small group discussion.
   a. Talk about and demonstrate how to make a Headband.
   b. Talk about and demonstrate how to fringe a circle.
   c. Pass out scissors and Teacher-Prepared Materials.
   d. Let children tell you what each piece of paper could become.

2. Child fringes the paper strip, then the circles.

3. Child chooses items from scrap box.

4. Child lays circles out on Headband, in a design that pleases the child.

5. Child sets up for gluing.

6. Child glues the circles and extra pieces onto Headband.

7. Child helps to clean up the work area.

8. Teacher measures Headband to fit child's head and staples Headband together.

Lion's Face

Supplies

Scissors
Glue
Paper Towels
Scrap Box

Procedure

1. Small group discussion.

a. Talk about lions; have pictures and models of lions.

b. Talk about each piece of paper and what part of the Lion it could be after the child cuts it.

c. Let children tell you other things they would like to make.

d. Pass out scissors and Teacher-Prepared Materials.

2. Child cuts paper pieces into the Lion's face.

a. Fringe 2" x 3" into Lion's mane.

b. Snip eyes, nose, ears and mouth.

Teacher-Prepared Materials

Paper Circle, 9" diameter (Head)(Child's name on back.)
Paper Strips, 2" x 3" (Mane)
Paper Strip 1l/2" x 4" (Eyes and Nose)
Paper Strip 2" x 4" (Ears)
Paper Strip, 1/2" x 3" (Mouth)

c. Choose any extras from scrap box.

3. Child lays out the Lion's face in a way that pleases him.

4. Child lays out independent pieces.

5. Set up for gluing.

6. Child glues:

a. mane around outside of Lion's head;

b. eyes, nose, mouth and ears to Lion's face.

c. child adds the extra pieces in any way that pleases him.

7. Child helps to clean up work area.

Note: Help children working independently to follow a routine: cut, lay out pieces and glue.

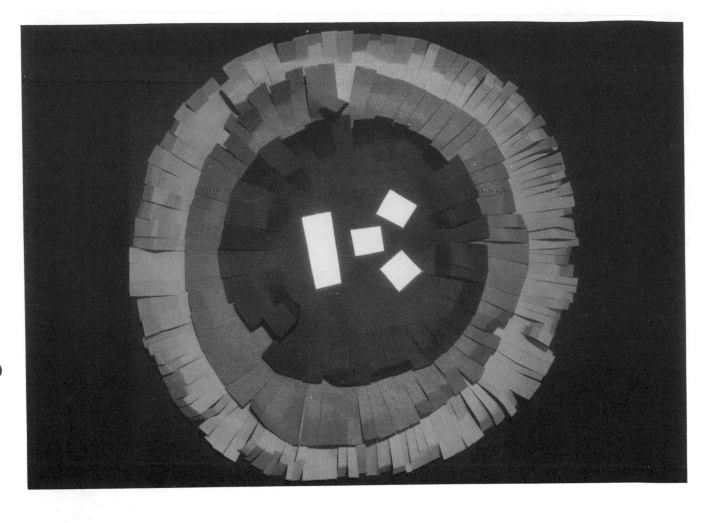

Porcupine

Supplies

Scissors
Glue
Paper Towels
Scrap Box

Teacher-Prepared Materials

Paper Circle, 9" diameter (Body) (Child's name on back.)
Paper Circle, 7 1/2" diameter (Body)
Paper Circle 6" diameter (Head)
Paper Strip 1/2" x 2 1/2" (Eyes, Nose and Mouth)

Procedure

1. Small group discussion.
a. Talk about porcupines; have pictures and models.
b. Talk about and demonstrate how to make a Porcupine.
c. Let children tell you other things they would like to make.
d. Pass out scissors and Teacher-Prepared Materials.
e. Let children tell you what each piece of paper will become.
f. Child may choose from scrap box.

2. Child cuts:
a. fringe paper circles for body and head;
b. snip paper strips for eyes, nose and mouth;
c. any additional pieces he wants.

3. Child lays out Porcupine in a way that pleases him.

4. Set up for gluing.

5. Child glues:
a. Body to head
b. Eyes, nose, mouth to head.

6. Child helps to clean up work area.

Note: Help children working independently to follow a routine: cut, lay out pieces and glue.

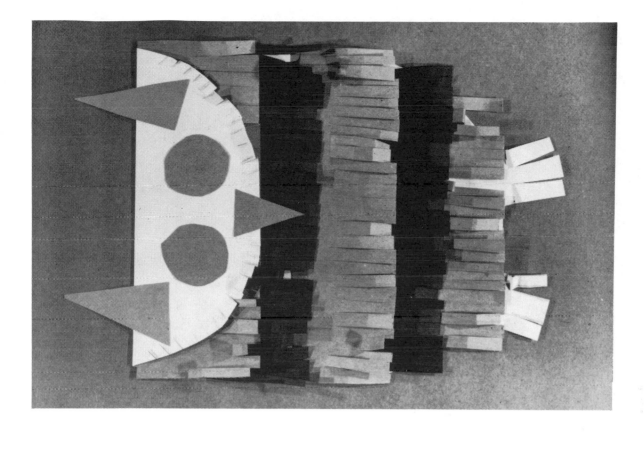

Owl

Supplies

Scissors
Glue
Paper Towels
Scrap Box

Teacher-Prepared Materials

5 Paper Strips, 2" x 6" (Feathers)
Paper Square 1" x 1" (Ears)
Paper Strip 1" x 2" (Feet)
Owl Shape 9" x 6" (Body); fold over top 1/3 of body to form head (Child's name on back.)

Procedure

1. Small group discussion.
a. Talk about owls; have pictures and models.
b. Talk about and demonstrate how to make an Owl.
c. Let children tell you other things they would like to make.
d. Pass out scissors and Teacher-Prepared Materials.
e. Let children tell you what each piece of paper could become.

2. Child cuts:
a. owl shape, fringe for feathers (on head);
b. 2" x 6" paper strips, fringe for feathers;
c. 1" x 2" paper strip, cut in 2 pieces and fringe for feet;
d. 1" x 1" square, snip on the diagonal to form triangles for ears.

3. Child lays out Owl in a way that pleases him. (Some feather strips may need shortening.)

4. Set up for gluing.

5. Child glues:
a. feathers to body (starting at the bottom of the Owl);
b. ears, eyes, beak and feet to Owl.

6. Child helps clean up.

Note: Help children working independently to follow a routine: cut, lay out pieces and glue.

51

Kachina

Supplies

Scissors
Glue
Paper Towels
Scrap Box

Teacher-Prepared Materials

2 Paper Strips, 2" x 18" (Feathers/Clothes)
Paper Rectangle, 1/2" X 3" (Eyes, Nose and Mouth)
Kachina Shape, 6" x 9" (Child's name on back.)

Procedure

1. Small group discussion.
   a. Talk about Kachinas; read or tell a Hopi Indian story.
   b. Let children tell their experiences with Hopi culture.
   c. Let children tell you other things they would like to make.
   d. Pass out scissors and Teacher-Prepared Materials.
   e. Let children tell you what each piece of paper will become.
   f. Let children find items from scrap box.

2. Child cuts:
   a. 2" x 18" paper strips, fringe for feathers/clothes, then snip in smaller pieces to fit on her Kachina;
   b. 1/2" x 3" paper strip, snipped into eyes, nose and mouth.

3. Child lays out her cut and extra pieces into a Kachina.

4. Set up for gluing.

5. Child glues:
   a. feathers/clothes on body, starting at feet and hands;
   b. eyes, nose and mouth onto face.

6. Child helps clean up.

Note: Help children working independently to follow a routine of: cut, lay out and glue.

Children's Ideas

Mrs Melton's
Head start Class

Children's Ideas

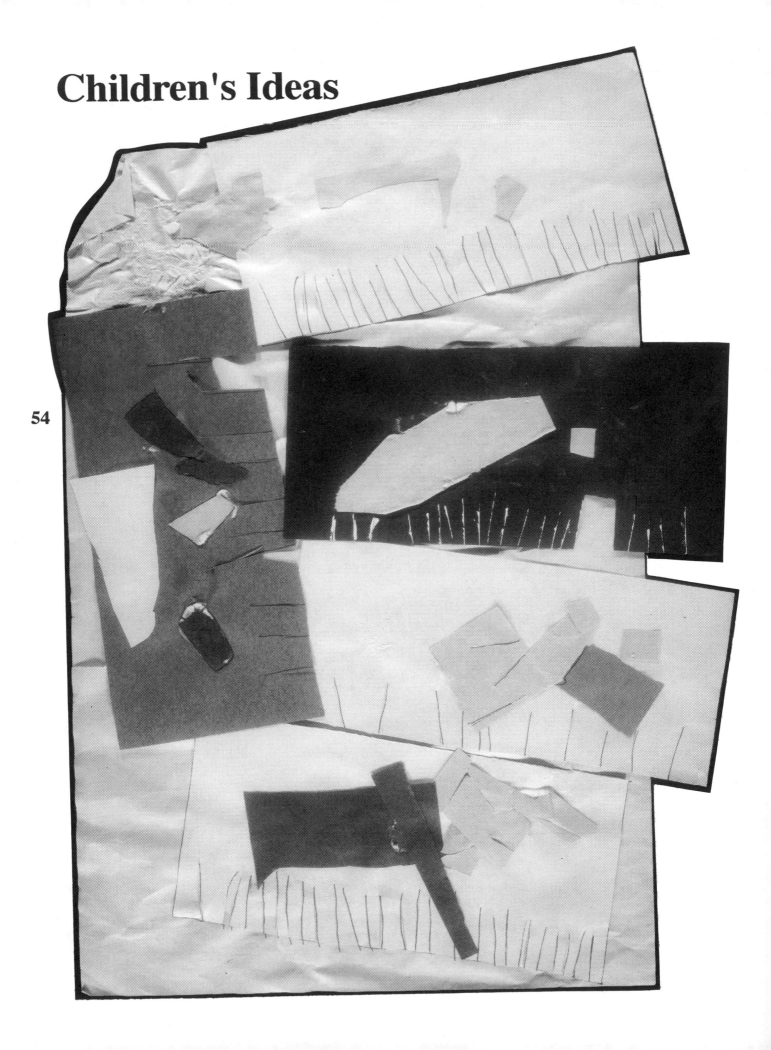

Teacher Ideas

1. Make strips available for children to use as they like.
2. Collage.
3. Other hairy or feathered animals.
4. Flowers.

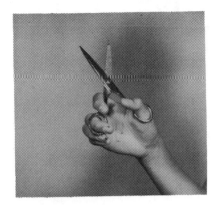

Skill Three

Strip

I. Instructions

A. Skill

1. Move the scissors through a length of paper.
2. Move the paper-holding hand in rhythm with the scissors.

B. Language

side	top	bottom
chew	slip	slide

C. Paper Rectangle

1. Materials - 6" to 8" long

                4" to 6" wide

2. Procedure
   a. Relaxed cutting position.
   b. Hold the strip so that the length is perpendicular to the body.
   c. The paper holding hand should be on the long side of the rectangle nearest it.
   d. Cutting begins on the side nearest the scissors hand and at the bottom of the paper. The motion of the scissors hand is only to open and close the scissors.
   e. The holding hand moves the paper into a cutting position.
   f. When the hands are about parallel, the cutting stops. The paper is held between the scissors blades and the paper holding hand moves away from the body and catches the paper at a place nearer the top of the paper. Cutting begins again.
   g. A natural rhythm of cut, slip, cut, slip — paper hand moves toward the top of the paper — is developed. .
   h. Scissors DO NOT close. (essential to cutting a smooth strip.)
   i. Scissors may close on final snip.

II. Problems and Solutions

A. Moving the paper into the scissors faster than the scissors can cut it.

1. Use any of the Use of Hands and Bilateral Integration activities (i.e., tearing paper, bead stringing, finger plays).
2. Rhythm activities are particularly helpful to help children learn to control the movement of their hands.
3. While using the scissors, an auditory clue of "chew, slip paper, chew, slip" may help to establish the child's rhythm for cutting.
4. Use of 6" x 6" paper square.
   a. The paper holding hand does not have to move.
   b. Place the child's paper holding hand in the middle of the side of the paper.

B. Feathering/Turtle Tails.

The scissors are closed, reopened, then move into the next cutting position or are just moved at the end of each cut. This results in a feathered edge - a series of turtle tails.

1. Return to the Use of Hands and Bilateral Integration activities.
2. Practice cutting a fringe to learn the stop action.
3. Verbal explanation to chew and slip rather than to close the scissors.
4. Use double-looped teaching scissors:
   a. teacher sits behind the child;
   b. child holds the paper;
   c. teacher and child hold the scissors.
   d. Child and teacher follow procedure outlined for this skill.

C. Left-hand child cuts away from mid-line.

1. Child moves paper-holding hand and scissors hand to the left side of his body (this is a directionality problem).
2. Return to snipping and fringing to help him develop a relaxed cutting posture.
3. Talk with him about keeping his work in front of his body. Continue to remind him in a positive way that this posture will make cutting easier for him.

D. Gluing paper strips into circles.

1. Child glues strip inside to inside.
2. Strip becomes a tear drop, rather than a circle.
3. Help child be proud of his developmental skill level. Continue to provide materials.
4. When child brings you a glued strip circle ask: "how does that make you feel?" Be pleased with the child.

Hairband

Supplies

Scissors
Glue
Paper Towels
Stapler
Scrap Box
Markers/Crayons

Teacher-Prepared Materials

4 Paper Rectangles, 6" x 8" (hair)
Paper Rectangle, 6" x 24" (Child's name on back.)

Procedure

1. Small group discussion.
   a. Talk about headbands.
   b. Talk about and demonstrate how to cut a strip and cutting posture.
   c. Pass out scissors and Teacher-Prepared Materials.
   d. Let children tell you about cutting a strip.
   e. Let children tell you other things they could make.
2. Child cuts rectangles into strips for hair.

3. Child decorates strips with markers/crayons.
4. Child lays out hair pieces onto Hairband.
5. Set up for gluing; glue hair pieces onto Hairband in a way that pleases the child.
6. Child adds individual materials from scrap box.
7. Child helps to clean up.
8. Teacher fits Hairband on child's head and staples ends together.

Note: Children working independently will cut, lay out and glue their creations.

Flowers

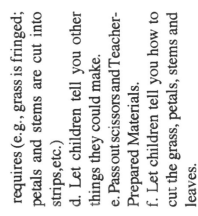

Supplies

Scissors
Glue
Paper Towels
Scrap Box
Local Flowers and Leaves

Teacher-Prepared Materials

2 Paper Rectangle 6" x 2" (Petals)
Paper Rectangle 6" x 3" (Stems & Leaves)
3 Paper Circles 2" diameter (Center)
Paper Strip, 3" x 12" (Grass)
Background Paper 9" x 12" (Child's name on back.)

Procedure

1. Small group discussion.
a. Talk about flowers and their parts. Have pictures and models of flowers.
b. Talk about each piece of paper and what part of the flower it may become.
c. Talk about and demonstrate the kind of cutting each piece requires (e.g., grass is fringed; petals and stems are cut into strips, etc.)
d. Let children tell you other things they could make.
e. Pass out scissors and Teacher-Prepared Materials.
f. Let children tell you how to cut the grass, petals, stems and leaves.

2. Child cuts:
a. 2" x 6" into strips for petals;
b. 3" x 6" into strips for stems and one strip into leaves;
c. 3" x 12" fringe for grass;
d. other pieces in ways that please her.

3. Child lays out cut pieces on background paper.

4. Set up for gluing; glue:
a. grass;
b. stems and leaves;
c. flower centers;
d. petals onto flower;
e. individual items she has selected and cut.

5. Child helps clean up.

Note: Children working independently will cut, layout and glue their creations.

59

Creepy Animal

Supplies

Scissors
Glue
Paper Towels
18" Yarn/String
Crayons/Markers
Scrap Box

Teacher-Prepared Materials

Paper Rectangle 6" x 8" (legs)
Paper Rectangle 4 1/2" x 6" (body)

Procedure

1. Small group discussion.
a. Talk about creepy animals.
b. Talk about and demonstrate cutting a strip.
c. Talk about and demonstrate how to tear small pieces off of the 4 1/2" x 6" body to give it shape.
d. Ask children what materials from the scrap box they would like to use.
e. Pass out scissors and Teacher-Prepared Materials.
f. Let children tell you how to cut the strips and tear the body.
g. Let children tell you other things to make.

2. Child tears rectangle for body.
3. Child finds pieces in the scrap box to use for project.
4. Child cuts rectangle into strips for legs.
5. Talk about and demonstrate how to fold the leg strips.
6. Child folds or rolls leg strips.
7. Child lays out her Creepy Animal.
8. Set up for gluing; glue:
a. legs to body;
b. string to body;
c. don't forget scrap box pieces.
9. Child helps clean up.
10. Child draws a face on her Creepy Animal.

Note: Children working independently will cut, lay out and glue their creations.

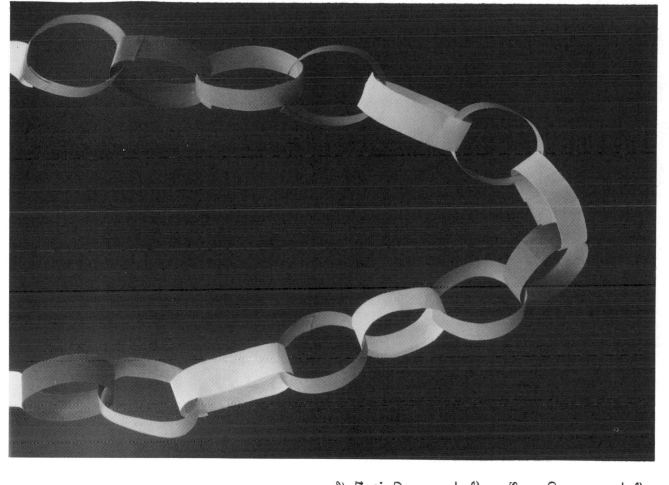

Paper Chain

Supplies

Scissors
Glue
Paper Towels
Scrap Box
Crayons/Markers

Teacher-Prepared Materials

10 Paper Rectangles, 6" x 8" (various colors)

Procedure

1. Small group discussion.
a. Talk about a paper chain.
b. Talk about and demonstrate how to cut a strip and how to make a paper chain.
c. Pass out scissors and Teacher-Prepared Materials.
d. Let children tell you how to cut a strip.
e. Let children tell what they will do with their pieces.
2. Child cuts paper rectangle into strips. Put child's name on one strip.
3. Child may use markers to decorate strips.
4. Child selects pieces from scrap box.

5. Talk about and demonstrate how to make the strip into a circle and how to link the circles.
6. Let children tell you how to link the Paper Chain.
7. Set up for gluing; glue:
a. one strip into a circle; (accept his way of putting the ends together.)
b. additional links; (accept his pattern for adding links.)
c. Add scrap decorations to chain.
8. Clean up.

Note: As children's math skills develop they will proudly show you the pattern of colors they have made.

Snow People

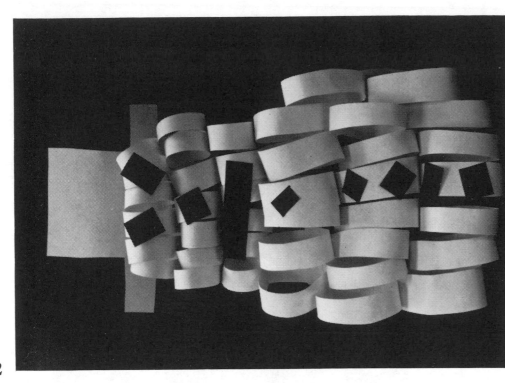

Supplies

Scissors
Glue
Paper Towels
Scrap Box

Teacher Prepared Materials

5 Paper Rectangles, 6" x 9" (3-D circles)
Paper Circle 9" diameter (body) (Child's name on back.)
Paper Circle 6" diameter (head)
Hat
Paper Strip 1" x 9" (eyes, nose, mouth and buttons)

Procedure

1. Small group discussion.
a. Talk about Snow People, have pictures, read story.
b. Listen to children's snow stories.
c. Talk about and demonstrate each piece of paper and what part of a Snow Person it could become.
d. Pass out scissors and Teacher-Prepared Materials.
e. Let children tell you how to make their Snow People.
f. Ask children what they will make with their pieces.

2. Child cuts:
a. 6" x 9" into 6" long strips for 3-D circles.
b. 1" x 9" snip for eyes, nose, mouth and buttons.
c. scrap pieces as he likes.

3. Talk about and demonstrate how to make 3-D circle.

4. Set up for gluing.

5. Let children tell you how to make a 3-D circle.

6. Child glues:
a. body, head and hat into a Snow Person shape.
b. all paper strips into paper circles. (Let children decide how to make their circles.)
c. all paper circles onto Snow person shape.
d. all pieces in a design that pleases him.

7. Child plans how eyes, nose, mouth, buttons and hat will be arranged on Snow Person.

8. Child glues these pieces on Snow Person.

9. Clean up.

Note: Children working independently will cut, lay out and glue their own creations.

Snails and Bugs

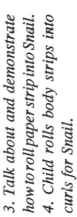

Supplies

Scissors
Glue
Paper Towels
Scrap Box

Teacher-Prepared Materials

Paper Rectangle, 6" x 12" (body)
Paper Scraps, (eyes, nose, mouth and antennas)

Procedure

1. *Small group discussion.*
   a. Talk about snails; have pictures, read a story, find Snails and Bugs in your playground.
   b. Talk about each piece of paper and demonstrate what it could become.
   c. Talk about and demonstrate how a wide strip will become a fat Snail and a narrow strip a skinny Snail.
   d. Pass out scissors and Teacher-Prepared Materials.
   e. Let children tell you what they'll make and what they'll need.

2. *Child cuts:*
   a. 6" x 12" into 12" strips for bodies;
   b. paper scraps into eyes, nose, mouth and antennas;
   c. paper in a way that pleases him.

3. *Talk about and demonstrate how to roll paper strip into Snail.*
4. *Child rolls body strips into curls for Snail.*
5. *Lay out Snail's face & additional pieces for gluing.*
6. *Set up for gluing.*

7. *Child glues:*
   a. face
   b. additional pieces onto Snail.
8. *Clean up.*

Note: Children working independently will: cut, lay out, and glue their creations.

63

Children's Ideas

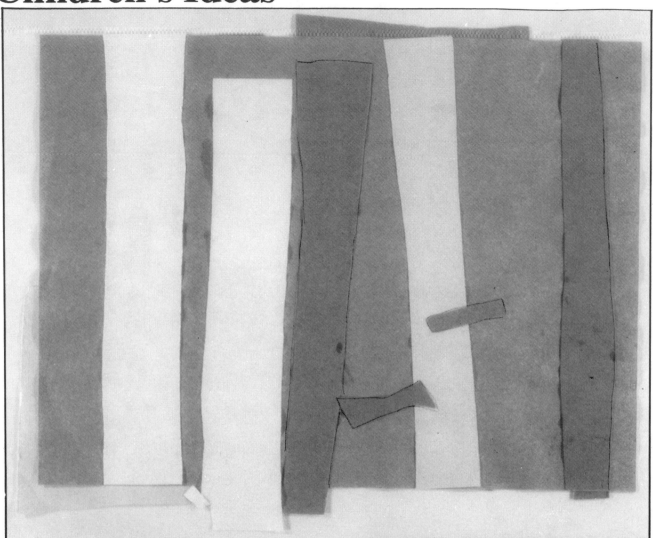

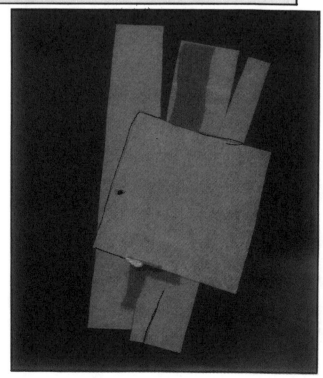

Children's Ideas

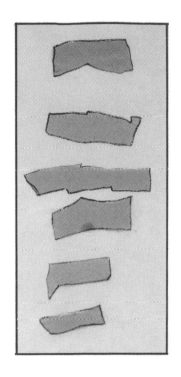

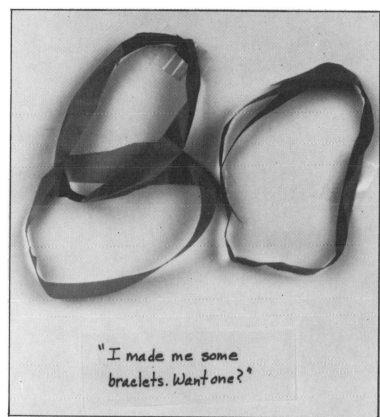

"I made me some braclets. Want one?"

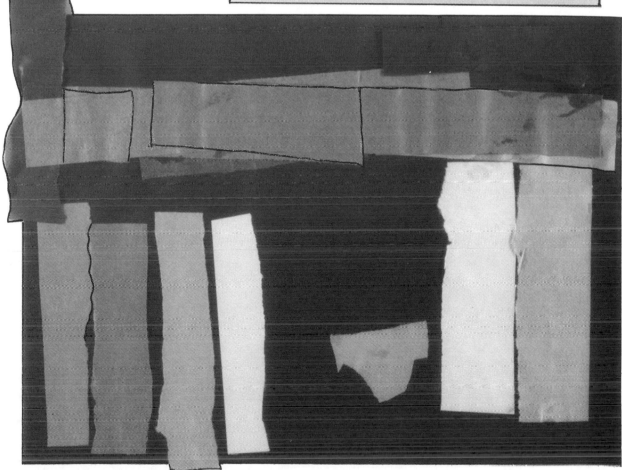

Teacher Ideas

1. Encourage children to bring in "scrap items" to class to cut and glue (be sure these materials are non-toxic before the children handle them.)
2. Use 3-D circles on other figures for door decorations.
3. See long tear activities.
4. Collage.
5. Watch your junk mail for interesting non-toxic paper for your children to cut in ways that please them.
6. Make a chain of tear drops and circles depending on each child's skill level and desires.

Skill Four

Sides

I. Instruction

NOTE: This is the first skill that the child is required to move the paper-holding hand and change the direction of the paper to cut a new area of the paper. Squares may be given to the child to discover this skill. Many three year olds need the straight edge to cut beside. Instructions for this skill: use a circle. Starting with a circle enables the child to see how she has changed the shape of the circle. By using a circle to teach the child to cut a side and angles, you make the task less difficult for the child. If given a square to cut a square, the child tends to forget where he started, so ends up cutting 6 or 7 or 8 sides. Given a circle, the child can tell when he has cut four sides. Cutting a large square into a small square, by cutting more than 4 sides will please children. Before and in conjunction with this step the child should have many experiences with angled shapes, as in II Problems D-1 -3 of this step.

A. Skill
1. Cut off paper side.
2. Turn paper to cut off an additional side.

B. Language

side	sides	square	triangle
rectangle	circle	like	shape
straight	edge	turn	

C. Square-like shape
1. Materials - Paper circle - Not larger than 8" in diameter - not smaller than 5" in diameter.
2. Procedure
   a. Relaxed cutting posture.
   b. Cutting begins near the bottom of circle near the scissors hand and continues to the top so that one side is cut off completely.
   c. Move the paper-holding hand towards the body. Catch the paper so that the newly-cut edge will be parallel to the body.
   d. Cut a straight edge towards the top of the circle.

e. The scissor hand and the holding hand return to their original position each time a new side is cut. The hands will find a natural rhythm of cutting and turning.

f. Scissors do not close while cutting the straight edge.

g. Scissors may close on final snip.

h. Verbally label the shape as square-like and the edge being cut as a straight edge.

D. Rectangle-like shape

Using an oval shape follow square directions to cut rectangles.

Label this new shapes as rectangle-like.

E. Triangle-like shape

Using circles as in C. Square-like -shapes and D. Rectangle-like-shapes modify those directions to cut three sides. Label the new shapes as triangle like.

F. Multi-sided shapes

Using the procedure learned to cut angles and straight edges, encourage the children to cut many-sided shapes. Use the traditional labels for these creative shapes when appropriate or encourage the children to make up new labels for their shapes.

G. Sided shape

1. Materials - paper pieces from Scrap Box.
2. Procedure - Encourage the children to change the shape of the piece of scrap paper and to label their shapes.

II. Problems and Solutions

A. Coordination of hands

1. See Skill Three.
2. Provide 5"x5" squares.
   a. Have the child cut off one side.
   b. Move the paper-holding hand.
   c. Cut off a new side.
   d. The number of sides cut off and the size of the final piece paper should be the child's decision.

B. Feathering

See Skill Three.

C. Excess paper hanging

Be sure the child cuts completely across the paper to eliminate the excess.

D. Cannot cut an angled shape

The child needs to have the feeling of angled shapes. This "feeling" comes through many varied gross and fine motor activities with angled shapes.

1. Gross Motor Activities
   a. Move in angled shapes (walk, crawl, run, roll)
   b. Move around, through, in, out of angled shapes.
   c. Paint angled shapes on court with water and paint brush, then with squeeze detergent bottles.
2. Fine Motor Activities
   a. Sorting angled shapes (big, little, color, size, labels).
   b. Play dough - make a "snake" and shape the outline of an angled shape.
   c. Use angled templates.
3. Language Activities
   Finding, verbally labeling, describing, verbally sorting angled shapes in his environment.

E. Follows the curved edge of the circle when cutting

Provide 5" x 5" squares
   a. Have the child cut off one side.
   b. Move the paper-holding hand.
   c. Cut off a new side.
   d. The number of sides cut off and the size of the final piece of paper should be the child's decision.

Headband

Supplies

Scissors
Glue
Paper Towels
Stapler
Scrap Book

Procedure

1. Small group discussion.
a. Talk about and demonstrate headbands and making up designs with paper pieces.
b. Talk about and demonstrate how to cut sides.
c. Talk about cutting posture.
d. Pass out scissors and Teacher-Prepared Materials.
e. Let children tell you about:
  1. cutting sides;
  2. cutting posture;
  3. making up a paper design;
  4. what they will make.

Teacher-Prepared Materials

5 Paper Circles, 4" diameter
5 Paper Ovals, 4" x 6" axis
5 pieces of Scrap Paper
Paper Strip 6" x 24" (Child's name on back.)

2. Child cuts:
  a. circles into squares;
  b. ovals into rectangles;
  c. scraps into sided shapes.
3. Lay out squares, rectangles and sided shapes on Headband.
4. Set up for gluing; glue shapes onto Headband in a way that pleases the child.
5. Clean up.
6. Teacher measures Headband to fit child's head and staples Headband together.

Note: Children may create independent ideas with these materials.

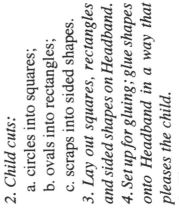

City

Supplies

Scissors
Glue
Paper Towels
Crayon/Markers
Scrap Box

Teacher-Prepared Materials

2 Paper Circles, 5" diameter (Buildings)
3 Paper Circles, 3" diameter (Buildings)
Paper Strip, 1/2" x 18" (Windows)
Background Paper, 9" x 12"
(Child's name on back.)

Procedure

1. Small group discussion.
a. Talk about cities (yours in particular); have pictures.
b. Talk about and demonstrate what each piece of paper could become. Be sure to show the children that the scrap pieces can be re-cut into grass, flowers, trees, etc.
c. Pass out scissors and Teacher-Prepared Materials.

d. Let children tell you:
  1. how to make their Cities;
  2. what they will make.
2. Child selects items from scrap box.
3. Child cuts:
  a. circles into buildings;
  b. strip into windows and doors;
  c. scraps into what pleases the child.

4. Child lays out City on background paper.
5. Set up for gluing; glue:
  a. buildings onto background paper;
  b. windows onto buildings;
  c. child's creation and scrap box items.

6. Clean up (except for crayons/markers).
7. Child adds drawing to City.

Note: Children may create independent ideas with these materials.

71

Small Creatures

Supplies

Scissors
Glue
Paper Towels
Scrap Box

Teacher-Prepared Materials

Paper Circle, 6" diameter (Body)
(Child's name center back.)
2 Paper Circles, 3" diameter (Ears)
Paper Strip, 1/2" x 5" (Tail and Eyes)
Paper Strip, 2" x 3" (Whiskers)

Procedure

1. Small group discussion.
a. Talk about mice and other small creatures; have pictures; learn a poem.
b. Talk about each piece of paper and demonstrate what it could become.

c. Pass out scissors and Teacher-Prepared Materials.
d. Let children tell you how to make their small creature or other ideas.

2. Child cuts:
a. paper circles into triangles for body and ear;
b. paper strips into tail, eyes and whiskers;
c. or as she plans.
3. Child lays out small creature.

4. Set up for gluing; glue:
a. ears onto body;
b. eyes, whiskers and tail onto body;
c. other pieces as she has planned.
5. Clean up.

Note: Children may create independent ideas using these materials.

3-D Collage

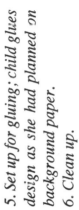

Supplies

Scissors
Glue
Paper Towels
Scrap Box

Teacher-Prepared Materials

2 Paper Circles, 6" diameter
2 Paper Circles, 3" diameter
Paper Strip, 1" x 12"
Paper Rectangle, 3" x 6"
Background Paper, 9" x 12" (Child's name on back.)

Procedure

1. Small group discussion.
a. Talk about designs and how to make them 3-D.
b. Talk about the paper pieces and demonstrate how to make them into 3-D shapes.
c. Pass out scissors and Teacher-Prepared Materials.
d. Let children tell you how to make a 3-D Collage.
e. Let children tell you what they would like to make.

2. Child cuts:
a. circles into squares (crumple up some for effect);
b. 1" x 12" strip into pieces;
c. 3" x 6" rectangle into strips;
d. scraps into what pleases her.

3. Child folds, curls, crumples to make cut pieces into 3-D shapes.

4. Child lays out 3-D design on background paper.

5. Set up for gluing; child glues design as she had planned on background paper.

6. Clean up.

Note: Children may create independent ideas with these materials.

73

Robot

Supplies

Scissors
Glue
Paper Towels
Scrap Box

Teacher-Prepared Materials

Paper Circle, 3" diameter (Head)
Paper Circle, 6" diameter (Body)
(Child's name in center back after child cuts the circle.)
Paper Rectangle 3" x 6" (Arms and Legs)

Procedure

1. Small group discussion.
a. Talk about robots; have pictures and models.
b. Talk about each piece of paper and demonstrate what it could become.
c. Pass out scissors and Teacher-Prepared Materials.
d. Let children tell you how to make a Robot.
e. Let children tell you what they would like to make.

2. Child cuts:
a. circles into head and body;
b. 3" x 6" rectangle into arms and legs;
c. scraps into antenna, feet, buttons, neck, eyes, nose and mouth.

3. Child lays out Robot.

4. Set up for gluing; glue:
a. body, neck and head together;
b. arms, legs and feet;
c. face, antenna and buttons;
d. other pieces they have invented.

5. Clean up.

Note: Children may create independent ideas with these materials.

Stick Puppet

Supplies

Scissors
Glue
Paper Towels
Tongue Depressors (Child's name in permanent marker.)
Crayons/Markers
Scrap Box

Teacher-Prepared Materials

Paper Circle, 8" diameter (Head)
Paper Strip, 2" x 9" (Hair)
Paper Scraps

Procedure

1. Small group discussion.
   a. Talk about what kind of puppet each child would like to make.
   b. Talk about each of the paper pieces and paper scraps and demonstrate what they could become.
   c. Pass out scissors and Teacher-Prepared Materials.
   d. Let children tell about the puppet they will make.
   e. Let children tell what they would like to make.
2. Child cuts:
   a. circle into head;
   b. strip into hair by snipping and/or fringing;
   c. odd pieces and scraps into what pleases him.
3. Child lays out Puppet.
4. Set up for gluing; glue:
   a. tongue depressors to head;
   b. hair to head;
   c. child's pieces to head.
5. Clean up (except for crayons/ markers.)
6. Child adds drawings to the Puppet.

Note: Children may create independent ideas with these materials.

Children's Ideas

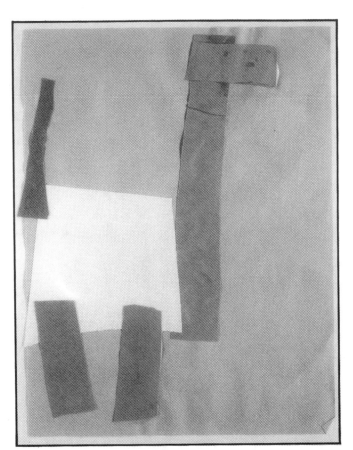

Teacher Ideas

1. Put out squares and circles. Encourage children to cut, move the paper-holding hand and the direction of the paper and cut again. Allow the child to cut the shapes to any size. The final shapes can be saved, glued or thrown away by the child.
2. Collage.
3. Cars, trains, planes.
4. Have children describe their shapes. Encourage your children to make up sorting and classification activities.

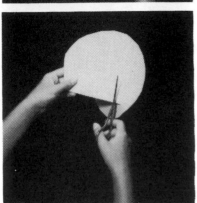

Skill Five

Angles

I. Instructions

NOTE: As in Skill Four a square may be used instead of a circle. Some of your children may acquire this skill by themselves during the sides instruction. Be sure they allow their scissors some turning room when they cut the angle.

A. Skill
1. Stop cutting near the edge of the paper.
2. Turn the paper allowing the scissors a quarter inch cutting room and continue cutting.

B. Language
angle   corner   cutting room

C. Square-like shape
1. Materials - Paper circle
   Not larger than 8" in diameter
   Not smaller than 5" in diameter
2. Procedure
   a. Relaxed cutting posture
   b. Cutting begins near the bottom of the paper and near the scissors hand. Continue to cut a quarter of an inch or so past where you want the corner to be. Do not cut the side off completely.
   c. Scissors blades hold paper.
   d. Move the paper-holding hand towards the body. Catch the paper so that the newly-cut edge will be about parallel to the body.
   e. Move scissors into cutting position allowing scissors room to begin cutting, and cut to the edge of the new side.
   f. Turn paper to easily snip off the excess paper.
   g. Continue to cut the side, again stopping about a quarter of an inch past the desired corner.
   h. Proceed as in c, d, e, f, and g, until a square is cut.
   i. Scissors do not close while cutting the straight edges.
   j. Scissors may close on final snip and when separating the square from excess paper.

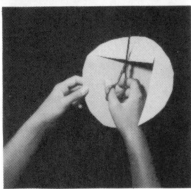
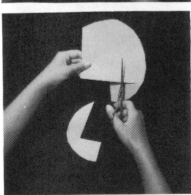

D. Rectangle-like shape

Using an oval shape, follow square directions to cut rectangles. Label these new shapes as rectangle-like.

E. Triangle-like shape

Using circles as in C. Square-like and D. Rectangle-like, modify these directions to cut three-sided shapes. Label these new shapes as triangle-like.

F. Multi-sided shape

G. Sided shape

1. Materials - paper pieces from scrapbox.
2. Procedure
   Encourage the children to change the shape of the piece of scrap paper and to label their shapes.

II. Problems and Solutions 79

A. Coordination of hands

1. (See Skill Three)
2. Provide 5"x5" squares.
   a. Have the child cut off one side.
   b. Move the paper-holding hand.
   c. Cut off a new side.
   d. The number of sides cut off and the size of the final piece of paper should be the child's decision.

B. Feathering/Turtle Tails

(See Skill Three)

C. Excess Paper Hanging

Be sure after the corner is cut that the child snips off the excess, if it gets in his way.

D. Follows the curved edge of the circle when cutting.

Provide 5" x 5" squares.
   a. Have the child cut off one side.
   b. Move the paper-holding hand.
   c. Cut off a new side.
   d. The number of sides cut off and the size of the final piece of paper should be the child's decision.

E. Cannot cut on corners

Walking, crawling, rolling up and down a slide or ramp to get the feeling of an angle.

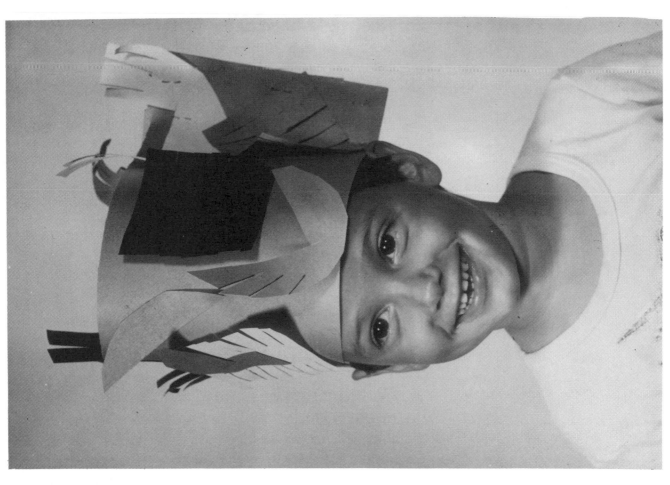

80

Headband

Supplies

Scissors
Glue
Paper Towels
Stapler
Scrap Box

Teacher-Prepared Materials

5 Paper Circles, 6" diameter
Paper Rectangle, 6" x 24"
Odd shapes of paper.
(Child's name on back.)

Procedure

1. Small group discussion.
a. Talk about headbands and have some examples of designs.
b. Have children tell about headbands they have made in the past.
c. Talk about and demonstrate turning the corner to cut an angle.
d. Pass out scissors and Teacher-Prepared Materials.
e. Let children tell you how to cut an angle.
f. Let children tell you what they would like to make.

2. Child cuts:
a. circles into squares;
b. fringes, squares and scraps;
c. pieces from Scrap Box.
3. Child lays out cut pieces and Scrap Box pieces on Headband.
4. Set up for gluing; glue pieces onto Headband in a way that pleases the child.
5. Clean up.
6. Teacher measures child's head and staples Headband together.

Note: Children may create independent ideas with these materials.

Wiggly Creatures

Supplies

Scissors
Glue
Paper Towels
Scrap Box

Teacher-Prepared Materials

10 Paper Circles, 3" diameter (Body)
Background Paper, 9" x 12" (Child's name on back.)

Procedure

1. Small group discussion.
a. Talk about snakes and
other wiggly creatures; have
pictures, read a story.
b. Talk about and demonstrate
how to cut a triangle.
c. Pass out scissors and
Teacher-Prepared Materials.
d. Let children tell you how to
cut a triangle.
e. Let children tell you what
they would like to make.
2. Child cuts:
a. circles into triangles;
b. scraps into eyes, tongue
and designs on Snake;

c. Scrap Box pieces as he likes.
*3. Child lays pieces out to make
Wiggly Creature.*
4. Set up for gluing; glue:
a. head onto background
paper;
b. body pieces onto back
ground;
c. eyes, tongue and design;
d. pieces as he plans.
5. Clean up.

Note: Children may create independent ideas with these materials.

Truck

Supplies

Scissors
Glue
Paper Towels
Crayons/Markers
Scrap Box

Teacher-Prepared Materials

Paper Circle, 4" diameter (Cab)
Paper Oval, 6" x 4" axis (Trailer)
Paper Strip, 1" x 6" (Wheels)
Background paper, 9" x 12"
(Child's name on back.)

Procedure

1. Small group discussion.
   a. Talk about trucks; have pictures and models.
   b. Talk about each piece of paper and demonstrate what it could become.
   c. Pass out scissors and Teacher-Prepared Materials.
   d. Let each child tell you how she will make her Truck.
   e. Let children tell you what they will make.

2. Child cuts:
   a. circle into square cab;
   b. oval into rectangular trailer;
   c. strip into square, then snips off corners for wheels;
   d. scraps into child's own creations as she has planned.

3. Child lays out Truck.

4. Set up for gluing; glue:
   a. cab to background paper;
   b. trailer to background paper;
   c. wheels to Truck;
   d. child's creations; as she has planned.
   f. items from Scrap Box.

5. Clean up (except for crayons/ markers.)

6. Child adds drawing to pictures when glue is dry.

Note: Children may create independent ideas with these materials.

Toys for Boys and Girls

Winter Landscape

Supplies

Scissors
Glue
Paper Towels
Styrofoam Cup
Hole Punch
Crayons/Markers
Scrap Box

Teacher-Prepared Materials

Paper oval 3" x 4" axis (Tree Trunk)
2 Paper Circles, 2" diameter (Sun)
4 Paper Circles, 3" diameter (House)
Paper Rectangle, 1" x 8" (Roof)
Background Paper, 9" x 12" (Child's name on back.)

Procedure

1. *Small group discussion.*
   a. Talk about snowy winters and where snow lands when it falls; have pictures, wait for a snowy day.
   b. Talk about each piece of paper and demonstrate what it could become.
   c. Pass out scissors and Teacher-Prepared Materials.
   d. Let each child tell you how he will make his Winter Landscape.
   e. Let children tell you what they will make.
2. *Child cuts:*
   a. 4" x 3" oval into tree trunk; uses scraps to cut branches and limbs;
   b. 2" circle into triangles for sun; uses scraps to cut sun's rays;
   c. 3" circle into blocks for house;
   d. 1" x 8" into 2 roof pieces;
   e. other pieces as he pleases.
3. *Child uses hole punch to make snowflakes from a styrofoam cup.* (If your hole punches are limited, you may want the children to do this in advance.)
4. *Child lays out Winter Landscape on background paper in a way that pleases her.*
5. *Set up for gluing; glue:*
   a. house to background paper;
   b. roof to house;
   c. sun to background paper;
   d. tree to background paper;
   e. snow to house and ground.
6. *Clean up (except for crayons/markers).*
7. *Child adds drawing to Winter Land when gluing is dry.*

Note: Children may create independent ideas with these materials.

83

Sailboat

Supplies

Scissors
Glue
Paper Towels
Crayons/Markers
Soda Straw
Scrap Box

Teacher-Prepared Materials

2 Paper Ovals, 6" x 4" axis (Sails)
Paper Rectangle, 9" x 3" (Boat)
Background Paper, 9" x 12"
(Child's name on back.)

Procedure

1. Small group discussion.
a. Talk about sailboats; have pictures and models.
b. Talk about each piece of paper and demonstrate what it could become.
c. Pass out scissors and Teacher-Prepared Materials.
d. Let child tell what she will make.

2. Child cuts:
a. 6" x 3" ovals into triangles for sails;
b. 9" x 3" rectangle into boat;

c. scraps into triangular waves for shark's fins and flags;
d. pieces as she pleases.

3. Child lays out:
a. sailboat (using soda straw for mast), waves and shark's fins on background paper;
b. child lays out project as she has planned.

4. Set up for gluing; glue:
a. boat onto background paper;
b. mast to boat;
c. sails to mast;
d. flags to boat and mast;
e. waves/shark to background paper;
f. rest of project as she planned.

5. Clean up, (except for crayons/markers).
6. Child adds drawings to pictures when glue is dry.

Note: Children may create independent ideas with these materials.

Shuttle and Rockets

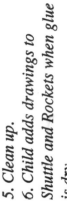

Supplies

Scissors
Glue
Paper Towels
Crayons/Markers
Scrap Box

Teacher-Prepared Materials

Paper Rectangle, 2" x 6" (Shuttle Body)

Paper Rectangle, 3" x 4" (Shuttle Wings)

Paper Rectangle, 3" x 9" (Main Rocket)

2 Paper Rectangles, 3" x 6" (Booster Rockets)

Procedure

1. Small group discussion.
a. Talk about the Shuttle; have pictures and models; watch a shuttle launch.
b. Talk about each piece of paper and demonstrate what it could become;
c. Pass out scissors and Teacher-Prepared Materials;
d. Let child tell you what he will make.

2. Child cuts:
a. angles off the end of the 2" x 6" rectangle to make nose cone for shuttle body;
b. diagonal across 3" x 4" rectangle to make shuttle wings;
c. angles off 3" x 9" rectangle to make main rocket;
d. angles off 3" x 6" rectangle to make booster rockets;
e. scrap pieces into rocket fire;
f. other pieces for his project.

3. Lay out:
a. shuttle and rockets;
b. his project.

4. Set up for gluing; glue:
a. main rocket to background paper;
b. booster rockets beside main rocket;
c. shuttle body to main rocket;
d. shuttle wings to shuttle;
e. fire to rockets;
f. other pieces as he has planned.

5. Clean up.
6. Child adds drawings to Shuttle and Rockets when glue is dry.

Note: Children may create independent ideas with these materials.

85

Children's Ideas

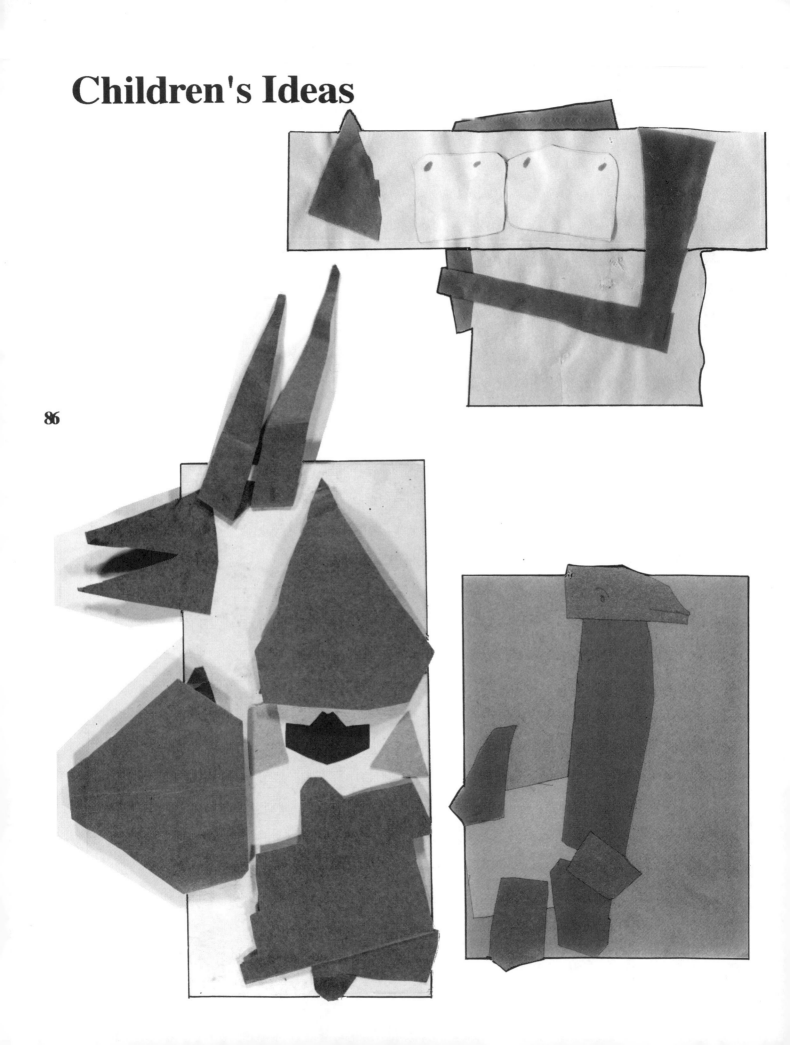

Children's Ideas

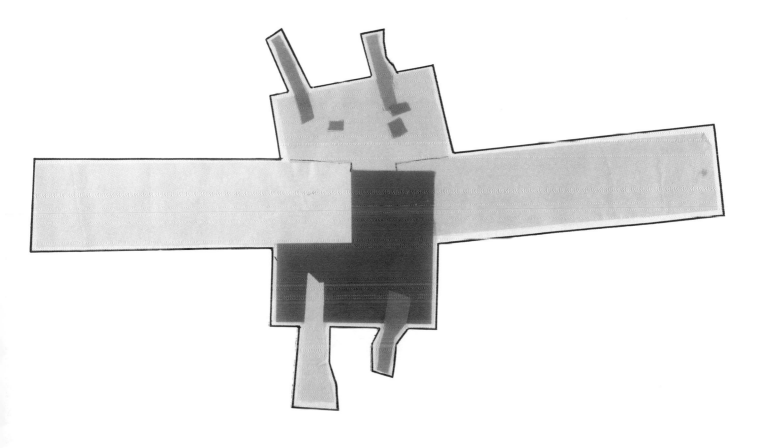

Teacher Ideas

1. Provide pre-cut paper, scissors, hole punch and stapler for children to create their own ideas. You decide how much adult supervision is needed for the children in your classroom to use these tools independently.
2. Survey your junk mail and packing materials for unusual textures for your children to cut. Be alert to chemical compounds on any materials you allow your children to cut. Always look for non-toxic labels on anything you put in your children's hands.
3. Your children will love cutting different materials. Many will be satisfied with the cutting and be content to throw away their cut pieces.

Turning
The Paper For Rounded Shapes

I. Instructions

NOTE: This step requires advanced bilateral integration.
Give the child many opportunities for success with activities that require each hand to make a different movement while the two hands are working together before introducing this step.

A. Skill

Turn the paper and cut at the same time.

B. Language

circle   oval   round   turn and cut

C. Materials

NOTE: Let child choose which size and shape is the easiest for him to use while learning this skill.

Paper Rectangles - 3" x 8", 6" x 8"
Paper Square - 3" x 3"
Paper Rectangle - 3" x 6" (Round off one end of the rectangle to make a curved end.)

D. Procedure

1. Relaxed cutting posture.
2. The hands and paper form a straight line parallel to the body, hand-paper-hand, with the scissors in the appropriate hand. The upper arms should remain near the sides of the body.
3. Cutting begins about 3" from the top corner opposite the paper-holding hand.
4. Turn the paper slowly so as to round off the corner.
5. The cut may end at the top of the rectangle or at the side opposite the beginning side.
6. Turn paper and begin on a new side.
7. The motion of the scissors hand is only cutting.
8. The motion of the paper-holding hand is turning the paper.
9. Verbally label the shape as circle-like.

NOTE: 1. When using a square, the child may cut a semi-circle and then want a new square. 2. Cutting and turning may be easier if the end of the rectangle has been rounded off.

II. Problems and Solutions

A. Cannot cut and turn the paper at the same time.

1. See Bilateral Integration & Bilateral Use of Hands, pages 4 & 5.
2. Provide plastic jars and tops for the child to screw together. Encourage him to hold one hand still while the second hand turns the top. Then turn both hands in opposite directions. This provides practice for a cut and turn pattern, which will develop a rhythm of cut and turn at the same time.
3. Provide 6"x 6" squares to cut square spirals.

B. Cannot cut a curved line.

As in Skill Four: Sides, provide gross and fine motor activities that will allow the child to develop a "feeling" for curves. Also use language activities as in Skill Four: Sides.

C. Perseveration of cutting and turning.

Getting lost in cutting so as to end up in a spiral.

NOTE: At this point the child did not intend to cut a spiral.
One of the skills being learned is a predetermined stopping point before cutting begins.

1. Point to and verbalize the stopping point before the cutting begins.
2. Draw half-inch lines from the side towards the middle of the square to indicate the starting and stopping points. This will give the child a general direction for guiding the scissors and is not intended to be a specific ending point.
3. Use the pointer finger of the cutting hand to trace the curve to be cut.
4. Give the child a 5" x 5" square with rounded corners to re-cut the rounded corners.
5. Use related activities for bilateral integration and bilateral use of hands.
6. Appreciate the child's current developmental level and encourage him to use his current skills.

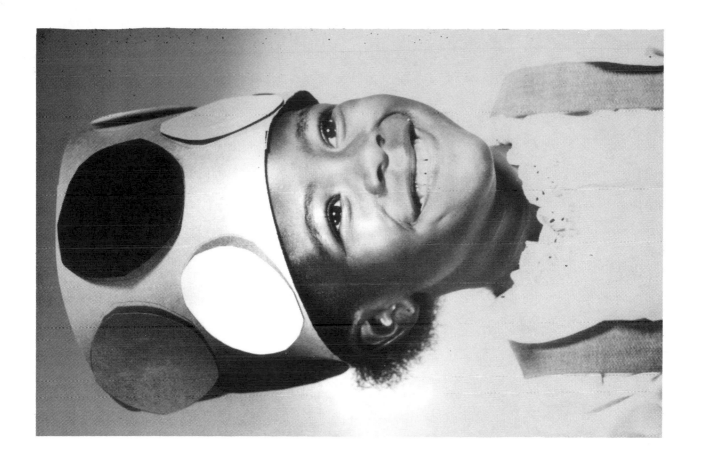

Headband

Supplies

Scissors
Glue
Paper Towels
Stapler
Scrap Box

Teacher-Prepared Materials

10 Paper Squares, 4" x 4"
Paper Strip, 6" x 24"
(Child's name on back.)

Procedure

1. Small group discussion.

a. Talk about cutting posture, especially keeping elbows at the sides;

b. Talk about turning the paper while closing scissors, cutting;

c. Talk about each piece of paper and demonstrate what it could become.

d. Pass out scissors and Teacher-Prepared Materials;

e. Let each child tell you about cutting curves and his project.

2. Child rounds square edges by cutting off the corners while turning the paper. (Some children may want to continue cutting with no interest in making a Headband.)

3. Lay out cut pieces on Headband.

4. Choose pieces from scrap box.

5. Set up for gluing; glue pieces on Headband.

6. Clean up.

7. Fit Headband to child's head and staple Headband together.

Note: Children may create independent ideas with these materials.

Elephant

Supplies

Scissors
Glue
Paper Towels
Scrap Box

Teacher-Prepared Materials

Paper Rectangle, 4" x 6" (Body)
Paper Rectangle, 3" x 4" (Head)
Paper Square, 2" x 2" (Ear)
Paper Strip, 1" x 12" (Legs, Tail, Trunk)
Background Paper, 9" x 12"
(Child's name on back.)

Procedure

1. Small group discussion.
  a. Talk about elephants; have pictures and models; read *Elmer.*
  b. Talk about each piece of paper and demonstrate what it may become.
  c. Talk about cutting and turning the paper to round the corners of the square.
  d. Pass out scissors and Teacher-Prepared Materials.

2. Child cuts:
  a. corners of 4" x 6" into curves for body (crumple up body for wrinkled effect);
  b. corners of 3" x 4" into curves for head;
  c. corners of 2" x 2" into curves for ears;
  d. 1" x 12" into legs, tail and trunk;
  e. let children tell you about:
      1. cutting curves;
      2. making an Elephant.
3. Lay out cut pieces to make the Elephant.

4. Set up for gluing; glue:
  a. body to background paper;
  b. head to body;
  c. ear to head;
  d. legs, trunk, Elephant.
5. Clean up.

Note: Children may create independent ideas with these materials.

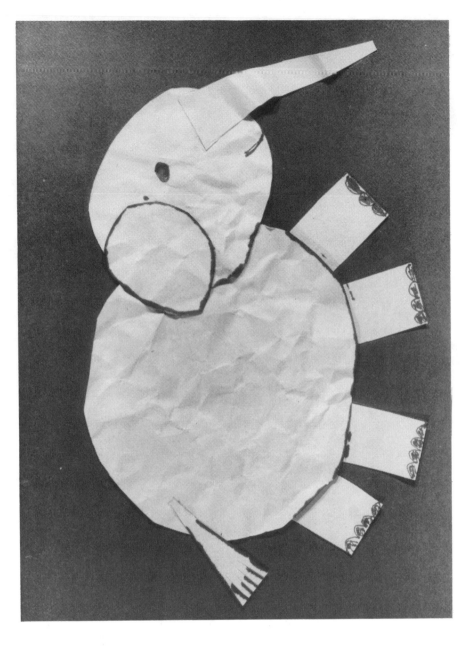

92

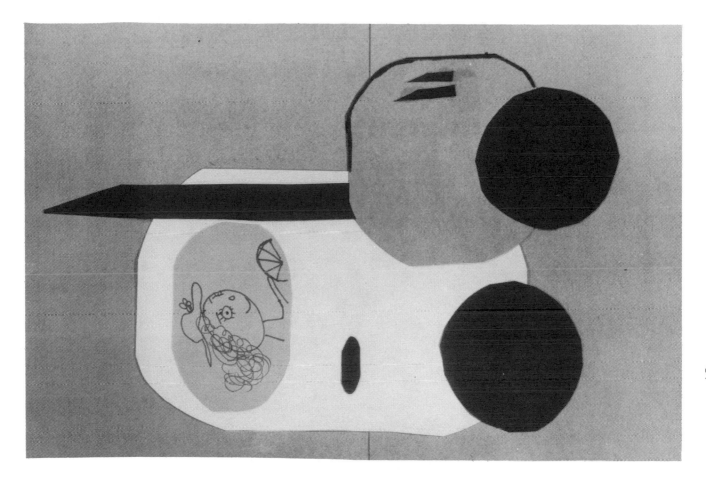

Car

Supplies

Scissors
Glue
Paper Towels
Crayons/Markers
Scrap Box

Procedure

1. Small group discussion.

a. Talk about the parts of a car; have pictures/models of cars; a puzzle that shows parts of a car.

b. Talk about each piece of paper and demonstrate what it could become.

c. Talk about turning the paper while cutting it.

d. Pass out scissors and Teacher-Prepared Materials.

e. Let child tell you about:

  1. cutting curves;

  2. making a Car;

  3. making their projects.

2. Child cuts:

a. 6" x 9" into body;

b. 3" x 3" into wheels;

c. 4" x 5" into hood;

Teacher-Prepared Materials

Paper Rectangle, 6" x 9" (Body)

Paper Squares, 3" x 3" (Wheels)

Paper Rectangle, 4" x 5" (Hood)

Paper Strip, 1/2" x 9"
(Antenna, Door Handles)

Paper Rectangle, 3" x 4"
(Window)

d. 3" x 4" into window;

e. 1/2" x 9" into antenna and door handle;

f. scraps into accessory pieces that please her.

3. Child lays out cut pieces into a Car.

4. Child lays out project as she has planned.

5. Set up for gluing; glue:

a. body and hood together;

b. wheels to Car;

c. window and antenna to Car;

d. accessory pieces to Car;

e. pieces as please her.

6. Clean up (except for crayons/markers).

7. Child adds drawings to her project.

Note: Children may create independent ideas with these materials.

Turtle

Supplies

Scissors
Hole Punch
Glue
Paper Towels
Crayons/Markers
Green Styrofoam Tray
Scrap Box

Teacher-Prepared Materials

Paper Rectangle, 6" x 12" (Shell)
  (Child's name in center.)
Paper Rectangle, 3" x 6" (Head)
Paper Strip, 3" x 6" (Tail and Legs)

Procedure

1. Small group discussion.
  a. Talk about turtles; have pictures/models.
  b. Talk about the hole punch and demonstrate how to use it.
  c. Talk about each piece and demonstrate what it could become.

  d. Pass out scissors and Teacher-Prepared Materials.
  e. Let each child tell you how to make his project.
2. Child punches circles out of styrofoam tray (this may be done ahead of time).

3. Child lays out pieces into Turtle.
4. Child lays out his pieces as he has planned.
5. Set up for gluing; glue:
  a. head to shell;
  b. legs and tail to shell;
  c. styrofoam dots to shell;
  e. other pieces as the child decides.

6. Clean up, except for crayons/markers).
7. Child draws on his project when glue is dry.

Note: Children may create independent ideas with these materials.

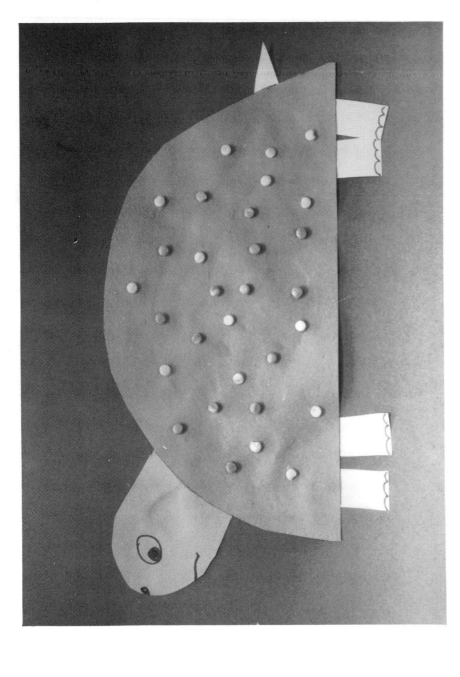

Peacock

Supplies

Scissors
Glue
Paper Towels
Crayons/Markers
Scrap Box

Teacher-Prepared Materials

Paper Square, 4" x 4" (Body)
Paper Rectangle, 4" x 12" (Tail Feathers)
Paper Rectangle, 1" x 3" (Head)
Paper Strip, 1" x 3" (Feet)

Procedure

1. Small group discussion.
a. Talk about peacocks; have pictures; a feather.
b. Talk about each piece of paper and demonstrate what it could become.
c. Slowly demonstrate cutting 4" x 12" into 2" x 4" feathers.
d. Pass out scissors and Teacher-Prepared Materials.
e. Let each child tell you how to make her project.

2. Child cuts:
a. 4" x 4" into body;
b. fringe body for body feathers;
c. fold 4" x 12" into 4" x 6":
  1. cut on fold;
  2. cut 4" x 6" into three 2" x 4" for feathers;
  3. fringe 2" x 4" for feathers.
d. 1" x 3" into head;
e. fold 1" x 3" into 1" x 1 1/2":
  1. cut on fold fringe 1" x 1 1/2" for feet.
f. other pieces for her project.

3. Child lays out:
a. pieces for Peacock;
b. pieces for her project.

4. Set up for gluing; glue:
a. head to body;
b. tail feathers to back of body;
c. feet to body;
d. pieces as she has planned.

5. Clean up (except for crayons/ markers).

6. Child adds drawings to project.

Note: Children may create independent ideas with these materials.

95

Clown

Supplies

Scissors
Glue
Paper Towels
Crayons/Markers
3 Yarn Strings 5" long
Scrap Box

Procedure

1. Small group discussion.

a. Talk about clowns, have pictures and models.

b. Talk about each piece and demonstrate what it could become.

c. Pass out scissors and Teacher-Prepared Materials.

d. Let each child tell you how to make her project.

2. Child cuts:

a. 5" x 9" into body;

b. 3" x 3" into head;

c. fold 4" x 6" into 3" x 4":

  1. cut on fold;

  2. 3" x 4" into 1 1/2" x 4" into arms and legs.

d. 3" x 3" into triangular hat; use scraps for hands;

e. 2" x 18" into approximately 2" x 2"s, then into dots;

Teacher-Prepared Materials

Paper Rectangle, 5" x 9" (Body)
Paper Square, 3" x 3" (Head)
2 Paper Rectangles, 4" x 6" (Arms and Legs)
Paper Square, 3" x 3" (Hat)
Paper Squares, 18" x 2" (Dots)
Paper Rectangle, 3" x 6" (Balloons)
Paper Rectangle, 6" x 3" (Hair)
Paper Square, 3" x 3" (Feet)
Background Paper, 12" x 18"
  (Child's name on back.)

f. 3" x 6" into approximately 2" x 3"s, then into balloons;

g. 3" x 6" into 3" x 3"s then, fringe for hair;

h. other scraps as she pleases.

3. Child lays out

a. pieces into a clown;

b. pieces as they please her.

4. Set up for gluing; glue:

a. head to body on background paper;

b. arms and legs to body;

c. hands and feet to arms and legs;

d. hair to head;

e. hat to hair;

f. dots to clown suit;

g. strings and balloons to background paper;

h. scraps as please the child;

i. other scraps as she has planned.

5. Clean up (except for crayons/ markers).

6. Child draws on her project.

Note: Children may create independent ideas with these materials.

Children's Ideas

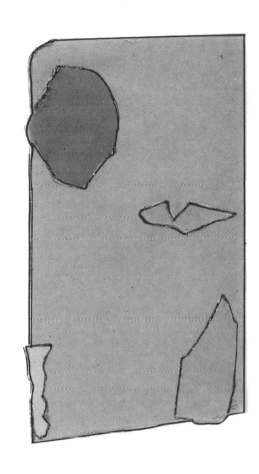

Children's Ideas

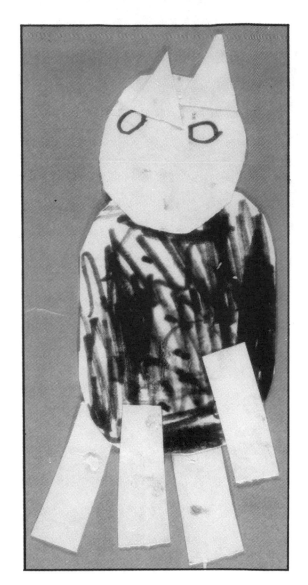

Teacher Ideas

1. Put out 2" x 2" squares, stamps, stamp pads and markers. See how long it takes for your children to discover how to make coins.
2. Collage from scraps and odd pieces.
3. Display pictures of other people collages.
4. Put paper craft books in your library area. Encourage your children to talk about the pictures.
5. Make new items available in your scrap box.

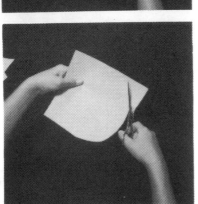

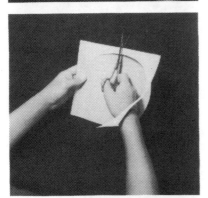

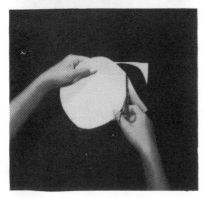

Skill Seven

Curves

I. Instructions

NOTE: Before and in conjunction with this step, provide activities of walking, drawing, crawling, sorting, finding, building with and talking about circles and ovals. (Use rope, stuffed stockings, string, macaroni, etc.)

A. Skill

1. Turn paper and cut in a circle shape.
2. Move paper-holding hand and scissors in a natural rhythm to cut curves.

B. Language

      curve   curves

C. Circle

1. Materials:
   Paper square 2" x 2"
   Paper square 4" x 4"
2. Procedure
   a. Relaxed cutting posture.
   b. The hands and paper form a straight line parallel to the body, hand-paper-hand, with the scissors in the appropriate hand. The upper arms should remain near the sides of the body.
   c. Cutting begins about half-way from the top corner of the side nearest the scissors-hand.
   d. Turn the paper slowly towards the scissors-hand.
   e. Cut towards the top of the square.
   f. The hands will find a natural rhythm of cutting and turning the square; snip off excess paper as needed.
   g. The job of the paper-holding hand is to turn the paper.
   h. The job of the scissors hand is to guide the scissors and to cut.
   i. The scissors' blades hold the paper when the paper-holding hand is changing positions.

D. Oval
1. Materials - Paper rectangle - not longer than 8"; not wider than 5"
2. Procedure -
   a. Start cutting on a short side of the rectangle.
   b. Proceed as in the circle.
      c. Because of the flat-side of the oval this will present a challange to the child. The turning of the paper changes in degree from the ends of the oval. So the child may end by cutting a straight line along the longest edge of the rectangle.

II. Problems and Solutions

A. Cannot cut and turn the paper at the same time
1. See Bilateral Integration & Bilateral Use of Hands, pages 4 & 5.
2. Provide plastic jars and tops for the child to screw together. Encourage him to hold one hand still while the second hand turns the top. Then turn both hands in opposite directions. This provides practice for a cut and turn pattern, which will develop a rhythm of cut and turn at the same time.
3. Give the child a circle 2" to 4" in diameter. The child will only be concerned with cutting and turning, not with the shape he is cutting. If a spiral results, allow for the success of turning and cutting. After this is mastered then see C. Cutting a spiral.

101

B. Cannot cut circle shape
Note: There is no standard for a perfect circle at this skill level. The task is to learn to turn the paper and cut at the same time, using a comfortable natural rhythm and cutting position.

As in Skill Four: Sides, use related activities to develop a "feeling" for circles. Also use language activities as in Skill Four: Sides.

C. Cutting a spiral
As in Skill Six, use lines and/or verbal clues to predetermine a stopping and starting point on the pre-cut circle.

D. Excess paper getting in the way
Cut it off at necessary intervals.

E. Uncoordinated use of hands and body
1. Hands turn in towards child's body.
2. Elbows raise up to almost shoulder height.
3. Task is too difficult. Encourage child to relax and cut in a way that pleases him.
4. Provide use of hands activities from the Chart to develop eye-hand coordination.
5. Encourage the child to cut in ways that please him, using his present cutting skills.

Buggy Headband

Supplies

Scissors
Glue
Paper Towels
Stapler
Scrap Box

Teacher-Prepared Materials

6 Paper Rectangles, 3" x 4" (Body)
5 Paper Squares, 3" x 3" (Spots)
Paper Rectangle, 3" x 6" (Legs)
Use scraps for Face
Paper Rectangle, 6" x 24" (Child's name on back.)

Procedure

1. Small group discussion.
a. Talk about bugs, have pictures.
b. Talk about cutting a continuous curve; i.e, turning the paper while cutting.
c. Talk about each piece and demonstrate what it could become.
d. Pass out scissors and Teacher-Prepared Materials.
e. Let each child tell you about:
  1. the bugs they have seen;
  2. making his Headband;
  3. what he will do with his paper pieces.

2. Child cuts:
a. 3" x 4" into body;
b. 3" x 3" into spots;
c. fold 3" x 6" into 3" x 3";

d. 3" x 3" into approximately 1/2" x 3" legs;
e. scraps into face;
f. pieces as he pleases.

3. Child lays out:
a. bug on Headband;
b. project as he has planned.

4. Set up for gluing; glue:
a. bodies on Headband;
b. spots on bodies;
c. legs on bodies;
d. face on head;
e. his project.

5. Clean up.

6. Teacher measures Headband to fit child's head, and staples Headband together.

Note: Children may create independent ideas with these materials.

Face Blowing Bubbles

Supplies

Scissors
Glue
Paper Towels
Soda Straw
4 Yarn Strings 6" long
Scrap Box

Teacher-Prepared Materials

Paper Square, 6" x 6" (Head)
Paper Squares, 1 1/2" x 3" (Eyes)
Paper Rectangle, 4" x 3" (Nose and Ears)
Paper Rectangle, 1" x 3" (Mouth)
Paper Strip, 1" x 8" (Hair)
Background Paper, 9" x 12" (Child's name on back.)

Procedure

1. Small group discussion.
a. Talk about faces; have children look at each others' faces.
b. Talk about each piece of paper and demonstrate what it could become.
c. Pass out scissors, soda straw, yarn pieces and Teacher Prepared Materials.

d. Let each child tell you about her project.
2. Child cuts:
a. 6" x 6" into head;
b. 1 1/2" x 2" into eyes;
c. 4" x 3" into 2" x 3" cut on fold;
d. 2" x 3" into nose;
e. fold 2" x 3", cut ears;
f. 1" x 3" into mouth;
g. 1" x 8" strip into 2 strips;
h. tear 1/2" x 8" pieces for hair;
i. other pieces for her project.
3. Child lays out:
a. cut pieces, soda straw and yarn on background paper;
b. pieces for her project.
4. Set up for gluing; glue:
a. head on background paper;
b. hair on head;
c. eyes, nose, mouth and ears on head;
d. soda straw;
e. yarn into bubbles;
f. the rest of her project.
5. Clean up.

Note: children may create independent ideas with these materials.

103

Vegetable Cartoon Character

Supplies

Scissors
Glue
Paper Towels
Crayons/Markers
Scrap Box

Teacher-Prepared Materials

Paper Rectangle, 8" x 9" (Body)
  (Child's name on back.)
Paper Rectangle, 8" x 9" (Arms and Legs)
Paper Square, 4" x 4" (Head)
Paper Strip,1" x 8" (Hair)
Use scraps for Hands and Feet

Procedure

1. Small group discussion.

a. Talk about vegetables and what makes them look like a cartoon character.

b. Talk about each piece of paper and demonstrate what it could become.

c. Pass out scissors and Teacher-Prepared Materials.

d. Let child tell you how to make his project.

2. Child cuts:

a. 8" x 9" into body;

b. fold 8" x 9" into 41/2" x 8":
  1. cut on fold;
  2. fold 4 1/2" x 8" into 4" x 4 1/2";
  3. cut on fold;

4. 4" x 41/2" into arms and legs.

c. 4" x 4" into head;

d. 1" x 8" into approximately 1" x 1 1/2" pieces;

e. fringe 1" x 11/2" for hair;

f. cut hands and feet from scraps;

g. his project.

3. Childs lays out:

a. vegetable cartoon character;

b. pieces as he plans.

4. Set up for gluing; glue:

a. head onto body;

b. arms and legs on body;

c. feet and hands on legs and arms;

d. hair onto head;

e. project pieces together.

5. Clean up, (except for crayons/markers).

6. Child draws on project.

Note: Children may create independent ideas with these materials.

Lamb

Supplies

Scissors
Glue
Paper Towels
Scrap Box

Teacher-Prepared Materials

Paper Rectangle, 4" x 6" (Body)
(Child's name on back.)
Paper Square, 3" x 3" (Head)
Paper Rectangle, 1" x 2" (Ear)
Paper Rectangle, 1" x 6" (Legs)
Newspaper Page (Wool)
Use scraps for Eyes, Nose and Mouth

Procedure

1. Small group discussion.
a. Talk about lambs; have pictures; models; learn poem.
b. Talk about each piece of paper and demonstrate what it could become.
c. Pass out scissors and Teacher-Prepared Materials.
d. Let each child tell you how to make his project.

2. Child cuts:
a. 4" x 6" into body;
b. 3" x 3" into head;
c. 1" x 2" into ear;
d. 1" x 6" into 4 legs;
e. use scraps for eyes, nose and mouth;
f. tear newspaper into 6" long and 1/2" to 1" wide strips;
g. pieces for his project.

3. Child lays out:
a. Lamb;
b. pieces as he planned.

4. Set up for gluing; glue:
a. legs and head onto body;
b. newspaper strips into circles;
c. newspaper circles onto lamb;
d. ear, eyes, nose and mouth onto Lamb;
e. his project pieces together.
5. Clean up.

Note: Children may create independent ideas with these materials.

Stand-up Child

Supplies

Scissors
Glue
Paper Towels
Crayons/Markers
Scrap Box

Teacher-Prepared Materials

Paper Rectangle, 3" x 4" (Body)
Paper Rectangle, 3" x 4" (Arms and Legs)
Paper Square, 2" x 2" (Head)
Paper Strip, 1" x 8" (Stand)
Paper Strip, 1/2" X 3" (Hair)

Procedure

1. Small group discussion.
 a. Talk about the children in the class and what special things make each one look and act differently.
 b. Talk about pre-cut pieces and demonstrate what they could become.
 c. Pass out scissors and Teacher-Prepared Materials.
 d. Let the child tell you how to make her project.

2. Child cuts:
 a. 3" x 4" into body;
 b. fold 3" x 4" into 2" x 3";
  1. cut on fold;
  2. 2" x 3" into 1" x 3" for arms and legs.
 c. 2" x 2" into head;
 d. tear or fringe 1/2" x 3" into hair;
 e. scraps into accessories that please her;
 f. other pieces into project parts.

3. Child lays out:
 a. Paper Child;
 b. her project as planned.
4. Set up for gluing; glue:
 a. body, arms, legs and head;
 b. hair and accessory pieces;
 c. fold 1" x 8" into triangle shape and glue together for stand;
 d. glue Child onto stand;
 e. her project pieces.

5. Clean up (except for crayons/ markers).
6. Child adds drawings to her project when glue is dry.

Note: Children may create independent ideas with these materials.

Underwater Mobile

Supplies

Scissors
Glue
Paper Towels
Crayons/Markers
Metal Coat Hanger bent into a circle
8 Threads 4" to 6" long
Scrap Box

Teacher-Prepared Materials

3 Paper Rectangle, 2" x 18" (Fish)
2 Paper Rectangle, 2" x 4" (Octopus)
4 Paper Rectangle, 3" x 5" (Seaweed)

Procedure

1. Small group discussion.
a. Talk about sea life; have pictures/models.
b. Talk about each piece of paper and demonstrate what it could become.
c. Pass out scissors and Teacher-Prepared Materials.
d. Let each child tell you how to make her project.

2. Child cuts:
a. 2" x 18" into smaller pieces for fish bodies and tails;
b. fringe for fish tails;
c. 2" x 4" into octopus; fringe for legs;
d. 3" x 5" into strips for seaweed;
e. fringe seaweed and crumple;
f. other scraps as desired.

3. Child lays out:
a. seascape in coat hanger frame;
b. her project as planned.

4. Set up for gluing; glue:
a. fish tail and body;
b. child adds his own cuttings as desired;
c. octopus, fish, seaweed to threads.

5. Clean up (except for crayons/markers).

6. Add drawings to project when glue is dry.

7. Tie strings to coat hanger and glue in place.

Note: Children may create independent ideas with these materials.

107

Children's Ideas

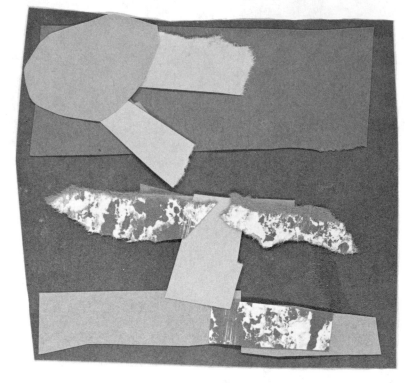

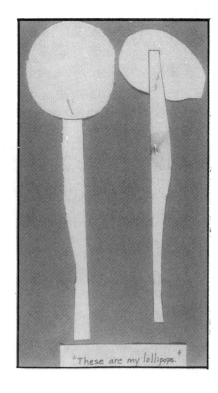

"These are my lollipops."

Children's Ideas

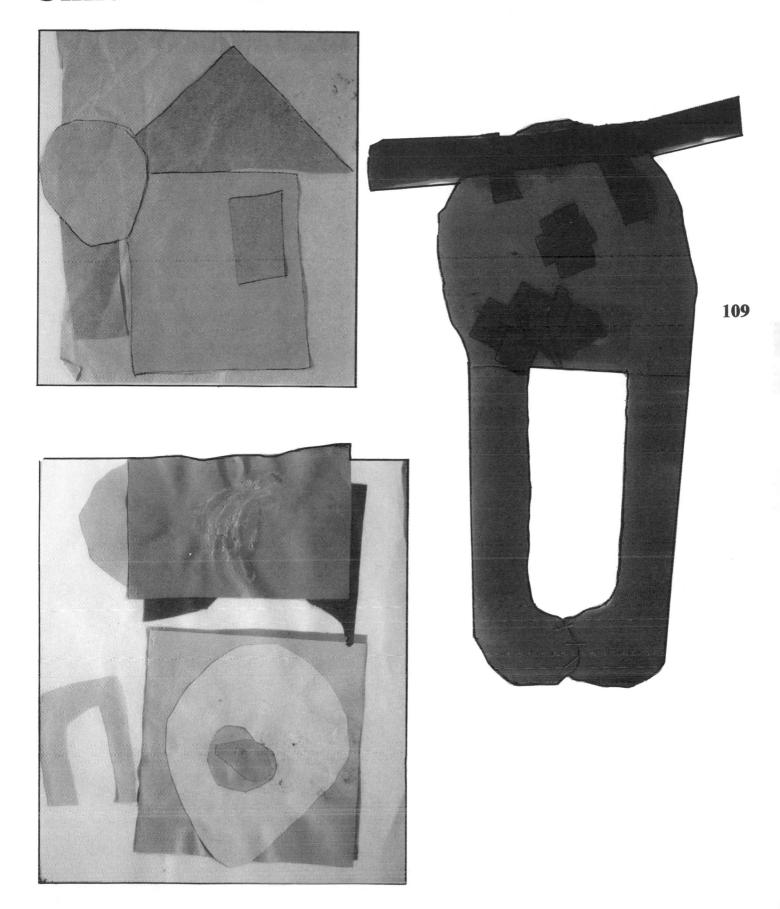

Teacher Ideas

1. Put out many sizes and colors of squares, rectangles and circles. Encourage your children to cut what pleases them.
2. Collage.
3. Happy/Sad Face.
4. Other Woolly Animals.
5. Stand-up People and Animals.
6. Other Fruit and Vegetable People.
7. Birds In A Cage (mobile).
8. Encourage your children to continue to use tearing in their creations.
9. Explore your classroom for things that have curves (not just circles and ovals). Have your children talk about and touch these items.

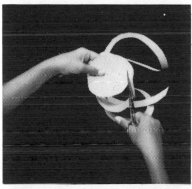

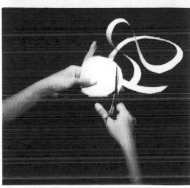

Skill Eight

Spiral

I. Instructions

A. Skill
Integration of Skills One through Seven.

B. Language
spiral cut into the middle of the circle
next to the side

C. Circle
Materials
Paper circle 4" to 6" in diameter

111

D. Procedure
1. Relaxed cutting posture.
2. The hands and paper form a straight line parallel to the body, hand-paper-hand, with the scissors in the appropriate hand. The upper arms should remain near the sides of the body.
3. Cutting begins about 3/4 of the way down from the top of the circle nearest the scissors-hand.
4. Turn the paper slowly towards the scissors-hand.
5. Hands will find a natural rhythm of turning and cutting.
6. Paper-holding hand turns the circle.
7. Scissors hand guides blades and cuts near the edge of the circle.
8. The scissors blades hold the paper while the paper-holding hand changes positions.
9. There is no perfect width for the spiral.

II. Problems and Solutions

A. Cannot cut the spiral
1. As in Skill Four, give the child related experiences to develop a "feeling" for a spiral.
2. Draw an imaginary spiral on the circle with the pointer finger of the childs scissors hand.

NOTE: A written spiral will complicate the task.

3. Let the child watch the teacher cut a spiral and then let the child examine the spiral.

B. Cuts the spiral piece so as to have only a smaller circle

1. Return to circle cutting for practice in turning, cutting, and guiding the paper.
2. Give the child a 6" x 6" square.
   a. Begin cutting at the bottom of the square.
   b. Cut a square spiral.
   c. Talk about cutting next to the side.
   d. After success with the square, return to the circle. Let the child tell you where he will cut to make the circle into a spiral.
3. This step introduces a new visual element. The child could have a visual perception problem.

C. Coordination of hands and arms.

1. Hands turn in towards child's body.
2. Elbows raise up to almost shoulder height.
3. Task is too difficult. Encourage child to relax and cut in a way that pleases him.
4. Provide use of hands activities from the Chart to develop eye-hand coordination.
5. Make materials available for the child to use his current cutting skills.

Mobile

Supplies

Scissors
Glue
Paper Towels
String, 16" long tied to
Paper Cardboard Strip, 2" x 8"
Scrap Box

Teacher-Prepared Materials

Paper Circles, 9" diameter

Procedure

1. Small group discussion.
a. Talk about how to cut a spiral.
b. Talk about only turning the paper and cutting with the scissors.
c. Talk about keeping the elbows close to the body.
d. Demonstrate how to cut a spiral.
e. Pass out scissors and Teacher-Prepared Materials.
f. Let children tell you how to cut a spiral.
g. Let children select items from Scrap Box.
2. Child cuts circles into spirals.
3. Child lays out Mobile.
4. Set up for gluing; glue spirals and other materials to cardboard.
5. Clean up.

Note: Children may create independent ideas with these materials.

Standing Collage

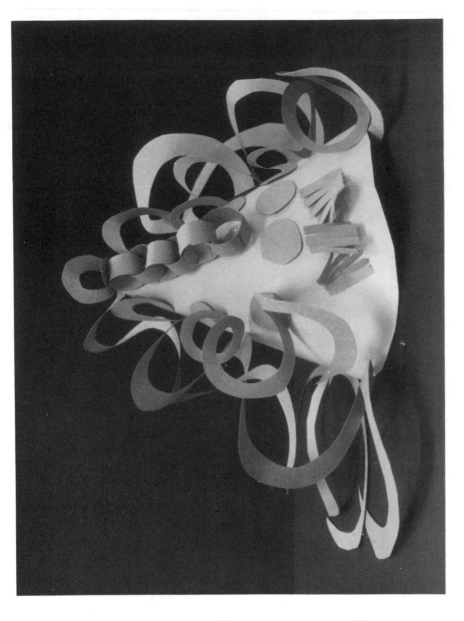

Supplies

Scissors
Glue
Paper Towels
Scrap Box

Teacher-Prepared Materials

3 Paper Circles, 5" diameter
3 Paper Circles, 3" diameter
Paper Strip, 1" x 8"
Scraps from previous projects
Paper semicircle from 9" x 12" sheet; overlap
and glue straight edges together to make a cone

Procedure

1. Small group discussion.

a. Talk about collage and planning a design.
b. Talk about how to cut a
spiral.
c. Talk about only turning the
paper and cutting with the
scissors.
d. Demonstrate how to cut a
spiral.
e. Talk about each piece of
paper and demonstrate what it
can become.
f. Pass out scissors and
Teacher-Prepared Materials.
g. Let children select items
from Scrap Box.
h. Let children tell you about:
1. how to cut a spiral.
2. how to make their project.

2. Child cuts:
a. all circles into spirals;
b. 1"x 18" into short strips;
c. scraps into what pleases the
child.

3. Child lays out design.

4. Set up for gluing; glue:
a. spirals onto cone;
b. strips into circles (chains);
c. child's creations onto cone.

5. Clean up.

Note: Children may create independent ideas with these materials.

Octopus

Supplies

Scissors
Glue
Paper Towels
Crayons/Markers
1 String 12" long
Scrap Box

Teacher-Prepared Materials

Paper Square, 9" x 9" (body) (Child's name on back)
8 Paper Circles, 5" diameter (legs)

Procedure

1. Small group discussion.
  a. Talk about octopuses; have pictures, model.
  b. Talk about how to cut a spiral.
  c. Talk about only turning the paper and cutting with the scissors.
  d. Demonstrate how to cut a spiral.
  e. Talk about each piece of paper and demonstrate what it could become.
  f. Pass out scissors, crayons/markers and Teacher-Prepared Materials.
  g. Let children tell you about:
    1. how to cut a spiral;
    2. how to make their projects.

2. Child cuts:
  a. **5"** circles into spirals for legs;
  b. **9" x 9"** into circle for body:
    1. draw eyes on body;
    2. crumple to get dome effect.

3. Child lays out his project.

4. Set up for gluing; glue:
  a. arms to body;
  b. string to body;
  c. his pieces as he planned.

5. Clean up.

Note: Children may create independent ideas with these materials.

115

Frog

Supplies

Scissors
Glue
Paper Towels
Crayons/Markers
Scrap Box

Teacher-Prepared Materials

Paper Rectangle, 6" x 7" (body)
(Child's name on back)
Paper Square, 4" x 4" (head)
Paper Strip, 3" x 7" (legs)
Paper Square, 2" x 2" (eyes)
Paper Circle, 5" diameter
(bounce)

Procedure

1. Small group discussion.
a. Talk about frogs; have pictures and models.
b. Talk about cutting a spiral.
c. Demonstrate cutting a spiral.
d. Talk about each piece of paper and demonstrate what it could become.
e. Pass out the scissors and Teacher-Prepared Materials.
f. Let children tell you
  1. how to cut a spiral;
  2. how to make their projects.

2. Child cuts:
a. 5" circle into spiral;
b. 6" x 7" into body;
c. 4" x 4" into head;
d. 3" x 7" into 4 legs; fold each leg after cutting;
e. 2" x 2" into 1" x 2"s into eyes;
f. scraps into additional decorations.

3. Child lays out project.

4. Set up for gluing; glue:
a. head to body;
b. legs to body;
c. eyes to head;
d. spiral to frog's back;
e. child's additional decorations.

5. Clean up.

Note: Children may create independent ideas with these materials.

Pig

Supplies

Scissors
Glue
Paper Towels
Brads
Scrap Box

Teacher-Prepared Materials

Paper Square, 9" x 9" (body)
Paper Square, 5" x 5" (head)
Paper Circle, 4" diameter (tail)
Paper Strip, 1" x 12" (legs and ears)
Paper Strip, 1" x 4" (eyes, nose and mouth)

Procedure

1. Class discussion.

a. Talk about pigs; have pictures/models; learn poem.

b. Talk about how to cut a spiral.

c. Talk about each piece of paper and demonstrate what it could become.

d. Pass out scissors and Teacher-Prepared Materials.

e. Let children tell you how to:

1. cut a spiral;
2. make their project.

2. Child cuts:

a. 4" into spiral tail;

b. 9" x 9" into body;

c. 5" x 5" into head;

d. 1" x 12" into 4 legs and 2 ears;

e. 1" x 4" into eyes and nose;

f. pieces as please her.

3. Child lays out project.

4. Set up for gluing. Glue:

a. head to body;

b. ears, eyes and nose to head;

c. tail to body;

d. brad legs to body for movable legs;

e. pieces as she planned.

5. Clean up.

Note: Children may create independent ideas with these materials.

Birthday Hat

Supplies

Scissors
Glue
Paper Towels
Stapler
Scrap Box

Teacher-Prepared Materials

One for each year:

Paper Circle(s), 5" diameter (spiral);

Paper Square(s), 4" x 4" (circle).

Paper Rectangle, 5" x ?" – 1" for each year (candle)

Paper Strip, 1" x ?" – 1" for each year (flame)

Paper Strip, 6" x 24" (child's name on back)

Procedure

1. Small group discussion:

a. Talk about Birthdays and this Hat.

b. Talk about each piece of paper and demonstrate what it could become.

c. Pass out scissors and Teacher-Prepared Materials.

d. Let children tell you how to make their projects.

2. Child cuts:

a. 5" circle(s) into spirals;

b. 4" x 4" into circles;

c. 5" x ?" into candles;

d. 1" x ?" into flames;

e. her pieces as she pleases.

3. Child lays out project.

4. Set up for gluing. Glue:

a. circles to headband;

b. candles onto circles;

c. spirals onto candles;

d. flames onto candles;

e. her pieces as she has planned.

5. Clean up.

6. Teacher measures headband to fit child's head and staples headband.

Note: Children may create independent ideas with these materials.

Children's Ideas

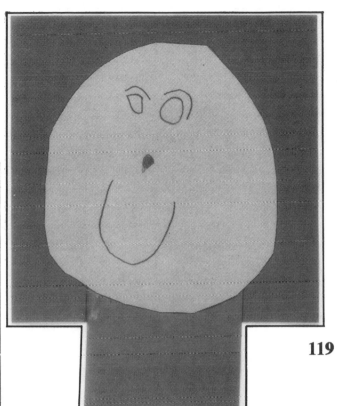

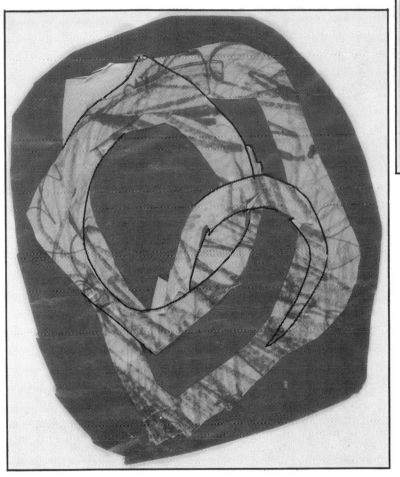

119

Children's Ideas

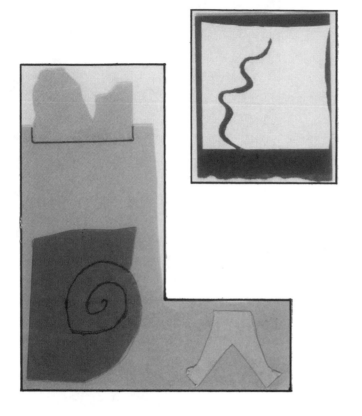

Teacher Ideas

1. Make many shapes of paper available for cutting spirals.
2. Collage.
3. Hairband (use paper plate for band).
4. Yo-Yo.
5. Snake.
6. Mouse.
7. Monkey
8. As your children experiment with paper they will discover than can turn the paper away from their mid-line and creat even more wonderful shapes.

Chapter Five

Line Cutting Sequence

For a child to follow lines while cutting, a new set of skills must be mastered. All of the areas of developmental growth must be refined. Naturally, visual perception and acuity play primary roles in the success of mastering the art of line cutting. During the mastery of these new skills, there are new problems which the child may encounter. These will be discussed and solutions given.

NOTE: For those of you who have turned to chapter five first because you think line cutting is easier.

Close observation of a child learning to cut reveals that cutting on a line complicates the task at hand. Following lines makes any task more complex. This is more obvious when thinking in terms of learning to ride a tricycle and/or bicycle. You would not require the child to follow a line in his initial experiences of learning to ride. Or, at a fine motor level, consider the initial use of crayons and/or pencils and the need for much "free hand" use of the

tool before lines are introduced. This sequence is based on child-tested research. Children have shown us that the best way to teach them scissoring skills is without lines to worry them. Go all the way back to tearing and, as you teach your children this sequence, teach it to yourself. You will be amazed at what you can "free cut."

Essentially the line cutting sequence is the same as the free cutting sequence. Following this sequence will help to reduce the difficulty of learning to line cut. The skills of Sides and Angles are combined, as are Turning the Paper and Curves, since these paper manipulation skills have already been learned.

Having mastered the free cutting skills, children at a pre-handwriting level will be able to draw the lines necessary to make these activities and will want to draw and cut their own creations. Encourage them to do so. In the beginning, the children may only cut around their drawings. Accept the way your children decide to "cut out" their drawings. As their skill level progresses your children will cut out more details.

The tools they will be using to draw their lines are: crayons, markers and/or pencils; with fingers, hands, rulers, straight edges and shape templates as guides. The children need instruction and practice time with these tools before they are required to use them for a cutting activity. Make these materials available in your art area so that your children can learn to use them.

Language continues to play an important role in learning to cut. When giving instruction for line cutting, use the phrase "cut beside the line" rather than "cut on the line." Cutting beside the line is easier. The line should run inside the top scissors blade, making it easier for the children to see what they are cutting. This puts the line next to the child's body and in his visual field. If a left-handed child uses a right-handed pair of scissors, he must look over the blade to see the line. If you are using Fiskars® for your left-handed children, give him the choice of using the Fiskars® or a left-handed pair of scissors so he can see the line more easily.

A child cannot take back a mistake made when cutting. This fact becomes even more obvious when applied to line cutting. Have plenty of scrap paper available for "tries". Encourage the child to throw away his mistakes and start anew or change his idea about what he was cutting. Please do not make him "live with it." After all, scrap paper surrounds us daily and, as the teacher, you have found a source of scrap paper for your classroom, so you have plenty of paper on hand. Place value on the positive development of a child rather than a single sheet of paper. When children are first learning to master line cutting, the accomplishment alone is "the end product," so any scrap paper suitable for cutting will satisfy their needs.

Free hand cutting is easier for most of us than free hand drawing. As children progress, they too, will cut far more complex creations than they can draw. (Examples: hearts, paper dolls, snowflakes, silhouettes.) Encourage them to continue to use their free cutting skills to add what pleases them to each activity. The activities for this chapter will include both free and line cutting.

Again the following format will be used:

1. A new skill will be introduced. Instruction will be given to the teacher for presentation to the child. Instructions for the left-handed child mirror those for the right-handed child.

2. Problems which may arise are listed and some solutions are given. Reference is made as to which developmental task from Chapter 1 should be provided to enhance developmental growth when required.

3. Activities are structured so that the children will become used to an organizational pattern for doing these activities. The organized child will then be able to use his energies on creativity within each activity, as he develops expressive language and visual perceptions of his world. The project directions are for the teacher's comfort level. Please note that the structure serves to give the child a sense of order to her work, NOT to dictate how each piece should be placed on the project. Helping the child to order her world allows her the freedom to express her creativity on each project. Remember, after you give the child the paper pieces they belong to her. She should decide how she wants to place them on her paper. Believe in her development and help her be proud of her present skill level.

Always have extra pre-cut pieces as well as your scrap box available for your children. This encourages them to make their own decisions about how their project should look.

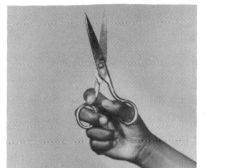

Skill One

Snip-Line

TO BEGIN THIS SKILL THE CHILD SHOULD BE ABLE TO FREE-CUT A SQUARE.

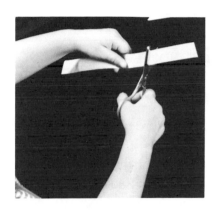

I. Instructions

NOTE: Before and in conjunction with line cutting, the children should have many and varied experiences with lines: walking, running, describing, crawling, again getting their bodies totally involved at both the gross and fine motor levels.

A. Skill
1. Placement of scissors in relation to the lines.
2. Maintaining the placement as he snips.

B. Language

line	on	beside	along
next to	follow	put	scissors blade
between	draw	two fingers	together
down	top	bottom	start
stop			

C. Materials
1. Paper Strips
   Length does not matter.
   Width 2/3's the length of scissors blade.
2. Pencil, Marker or Crayon.
3. The child draws bold lines from top to bottom down the length of the strip at irregular intervals of 1 to 1 1/2 inches. (You may want to ask the children to use their two fingers of the non-drawing hand to space the lines).
4. Newsprint to protect the child's desk from drawing marks.

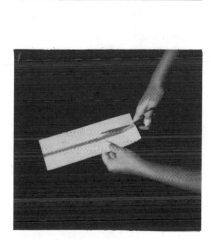

D. Procedure

NOTE: Please refer to the free-cutting photos for visual sequence.
1. Relaxed cutting posture.
2. Line placement:
   a. a right-handed child using right-handed scissors places the line inside the scissors blade, next to the body.
   b. a left-handed child using left-handed scissors places the line inside the scissors blade next to the body. HOWEVER, if the left-handed child is using a right-handed scissors, the line appears behind the scissors blade, not next to the body. This makes the skill more complex.
3. One snip is required to cut off a piece of the paper strip.
4. Scissors close.

II. Problems and Solutions

A. Cannot cut along the line.
1. Make all of the "scissors checks" to insure proper function and use of the scissors.
2. Begin with thicker/wider lines that are further apart. As the child has success, make the lines narrower and closer together. *(Note: a line wider than 1/8 inch is no help.)*
3. Provide activities so that the child can experience lines through his body: walking, crawling, rolling, running, etc., at the gross motor level; drawing painting (brush and finger), drawing lines in sand, sorting, etc. at the fine motor level.
4. String beads, put small pegs into peg board, give the child practice with eye-hand coordination.
5. Have the child draw the line on the paper strip:
   a. using the pointer finger of the scissors hand,
   b. the child traces each drawn line,
   c. then cuts that line.
6. Left-handed children will be more at ease and successful using left-handed scissors. The placement of the line behind the scissors blade makes the task more difficult.
7. Give child perforated stamps for child to cut along perforations. Each hole will provide a kinestethic reinforcement of staying on a line. (You receive these in your junk mail.)
8. Allow the child to continue to develop free cutting skills, giving him time to develop a readiness for line cutting.

Note: Because the child is drawing his own line, he may not need a "perfect cut." Let each child judge the "correctness" of his cut. Given self-directed cutting experience, most children will learn to follow the line when snipping.

B. Eyes

NOTE: A child with eye problems may "get by" while free cutting. In fact blind children can learn all the free cutting skills. Return him to free cutting and watch his eyes more carefully.

1. Make the following observations of the child throughout the day:
   a. Does he:
   1. run into things and people
   2. have difficulty identifying objects and people across the room
   3. hold things close to his face to see them
   4. have little control of his eyes (his eyes turn in or out at any time)
   5. have red or watering eyes
   6. have encrusted eyelids
   7. have frequent sties
   8. have swollen eyes
   9. adjust his head frequently while looking at distant objects
   10. have focusing difficulties
   11. have tracking difficulties
   12. rub his eyes frequently
   13. complain of itching, scratching, or stinging eyes
   14. avoid close work
   15. frequently blink, frown or scowl
   16. tilt or turn head to focus on an object
   17. tire after visual tasks
   18. move head rather than eyes while looking at a page
   19. frequently confuse similarly-shaped letters, words, numbers or objects
   20. cover one eye to sight with the other eye
   21. move clumsily or awkwardly
   22. have poor eye-hand coordination
   23. have headaches or nausea after a close visual task?

Adapted from: Garwood, S. Gray - EducatingYoung Handicapped Children: A Developmental Approach; Aspen 1979; Germantown,Md.

2. Make a referral for a complete eye examination.
3. Make a referral for learning disabilities testing.

Headband

Supplies

Scissors
Glue
Paper Towels
Yarn 40" long
Pencil/Crayons/Markers
Newsprint

Teacher-Prepared Materials

6 Paper Strips, 1" x 12"
Paper Strip, 6" x 24"
(Child's name on back.)

Procedure

1. Small group discussion.
a. Talk about and demonstrate using a finger or fingers to space the lines; and how wide spaces will make wide pieces and narrow spaces will make narrow pieces.

b. Talk about and demonstrate placing the line on the inside of the scissors' blade for cutting.

c. Talk about and demonstrate making a design on the Headband, using the yarn and cut pieces.

d. Pass out scissors, newsprint and Teacher-Prepared Materials.

e. Let children tell you:
1. how to use their fingers for spacing;
2. how to make wide and narrow pieces;
3. how to make their Headband;
4. ideas they have for their paper pieces.

2. Child draws vertical lines on the 6 paper strips using finger(s) for spacing lines. (Place newsprint under paper strips to protect the child's desk from pencil marks.)

3. Child cuts lined paper strip.

4. Child lays out design on Headband.

5. Set up for gluing; glue:
a. yarn on headband;
b. paper pieces onto yarn and Headband.

6. Clean up.

7. Child measures Headband to fit his head and staples Headband.

Buildings

Supplies

Scissors
Glue
Paper Towels
3 Small Boxes
Scrap Box

Teacher-Prepared Materials

3 Paper Strips, 2/3 the length of the scissors blade x 12" long (Windows and Doors)
3 Paper Rectangles to wrap around the boxes (Teacher could cover each box.)

Procedure

1. Small group discussion.
a. Talk about buildings and how they look.
b. Talk about the buildings in your neighborhood.
c. Talk about how to make a building.
d. Let children tell their ideas of how to use these materials.
e. Pass out scissors and Teacher-Prepared Materials except for covered boxes.
2. Child draws vertical lines on the 3 paper strips using finger(s) for spacing lines. (Place newsprint under paper strips to protect child's desk from pencil marks.)

3. Child snips paper strips into Windows and Doors.
4. Pass out scissors, newspaper and Teacher-Prepared Materials.
5. Talk about and demonstrate gluing windows and doors on Buildings.
6. Child sets up work area for gluing.
7. Child glues window and doors on cover boxes in a way that pleases him.
8. Child helps to clean up work area.

Note: Children may create independent ideas with these materials.

129

Horse's Head

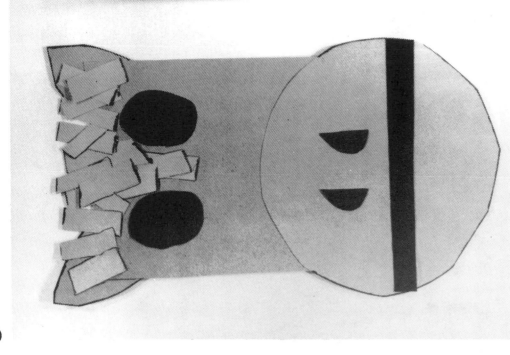

Supplies

Scissors
Glue
Paper Towels
Pencils/Crayons/Markers
Newprint
Scrap Box

Teacher-Prepared Materials

Paper Strip, 1" x 12" (Mane)
6" x 6" Square, (Nose)
5" x 6" Rectangle, (Head)
(Child's name on back.)
1 1/2" x 2" Paper Strip, (Eyes)
1/2" x 2" Paper Strip, (Nostrils)
1/2" x 6" Paper Strip, (Mouth)

Procedure

1. Small group discussion.
a. Talk about horses; have pictures/models.
b. Talk about each piece of paper and demonstrate what it could become.
c. Pass out scissors and Teacher-Prepared Materials.
d. Let children tell you how to make a Horse's Head.
e. Let children tell you their plans for these materials.
2. Child draws vertical lines on paper strip for mane. (Newsprint to protect child's desk.)

3. Child cuts:
a. lined strip into mane;
b. 6" x 6" into circle for nose;
c. nose scraps into triangles for ears;
d. fold 1 1/2 " x 2" into 1 1/2" x 1":
  1. cut on fold;
  2. 1 1/2" x 1" into circles for eyes.
e. fold 1/2" x 2" into 1/2" x 1":
  1. cut on fold;
  2. 1/2" x 1" into semicircles for nostrils.

f. 1/2" x 6" into mouth.
4. Child lays out cut pieces into Horse's Head.
5. Set up for gluing; glue:
a. nose to head;
b. mane to head;
c. ears, eyes, nose;
d. mouth to head.
6. Clean up.

Note: Children may create independent ideas with these materials.

Drawn Collage

Supplies

Scissors
Glue
Paper Towels
Pencils/Crayons/Markers
Newsprint
Scrap Box

Teacher-Prepared Materials

4 Paper Strips, 1" x 12" (Egg)
Paper Strip, 1" x 12" (Eyes, Nose, Mouth)
Paper Strip, 2" x 12" (Arms and Legs)
Background Paper, 9" x 12" (Childs name on back.)

Procedure

Note: These directions are for a Humpty Dumpty. Encourage your children to draw what pleases them; perhaps a scribble design.

1. Small group discussion.
   a. Talk about Humpty Dumpty; learn rhyme.
   b. Talk about and demonstrate how to make a Humpty Dumpty.
   c. Let the children tell you how they will make their project.
2. Child draws lines on 1" x 12" paper strips. (Newsprint under strip to protect desk from pencil marks).
3. Child snips beside lines to make pieces to fill in the drawing.

4. Pass out background paper and have child draw oval or other design.
5. Talk about and demonstrate using glue.
6. Child sets up work area for gluing.
7. Child glues:
   a. torn pieces onto drawn shape;
   b. torn eyes, nose, mouth onto shape;
   c. precut arms and legs onto shape.
8. Child helps clean up.

Note: Children may create independent ideas with these materials.

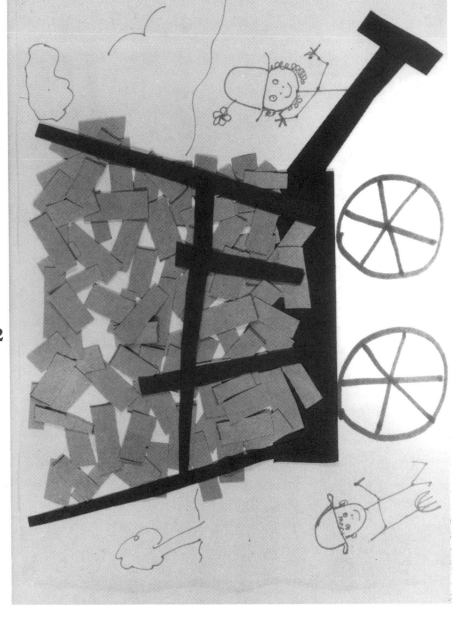

Haywagon

Supplies

Scissors
Glue
Paper Towels
Pencil/Crayons/Markers
Newsprint
Scrap Box

Teacher-Prepared Materials

4 Paper Strips, 1" x 12" (Hay)
Paper Strip, 11/2" x 12"
(Wagon Base, Wagon Sides,
Wagon Tongue)
Background Paper, 9" x 12"
(Child's name on back.)

Procedure

1.Small group discussion.
a. Talk about haywagons;
have pictures.
b. Talk about cutting hay
and cutting the 1" x 12" strip
into wagon base, sides and
tongue.
c. Pass out scissors and
Teacher-Prepared Materials.

d. Let children tell you:
1. how to make a
Haywagon;
2. what they will make
with their paper pieces.
*2. Child draws vertical lines
on the hay strips. (Use newsprint to protect child's desk.)
The wagon pieces will be free
cut.*

3. Child cuts:
a. marked strips into hay;
b. fold 11/2" x 12" to 11/2" x
6";
c. cut on the fold;
d. 11/2" x 6" into five 6" long
strips;
e. cut 6" strips to length for
wagon sides and tongue.
*4. Lay out Haywagon includ-
ing items from Scrap Box.*

5. Set up for gluing; glue:
a. wagon base on 9" x 12";
b. hay on wagon base;
c. wagon sides and tongue;
*6. Clean up (except for cray-
ons & markers.)*
*7. Child adds drawings to
picture.*

Note: Children may create independent ideas with these materials.

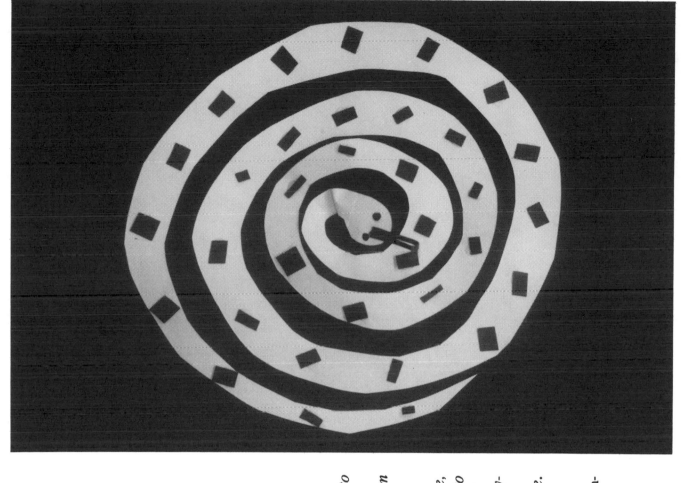

133

Snake

Supplies

Scissors
Glue
Paper Towels
Pencil/Crayons
Newsprint
Scrap Box

Teacher Prepared Materials

Paper Strip, 1" x 12"
Paper Circle, 9" diameter

Procedure

1. Small group discussion.
a. Talk about snakes; learn a song or poem.
b. Talk about designs on snakes.
c. Talk about and demonstrate cutting a spiral.
d. Pass out supplies and Teacher Prepared Materials.
e. Let children tell you:
  1. how to make their Snake;
  2. how to cut a spiral.
  3. what they will make with their paper pieces.
2. Child cuts circle into spiral.
3. Child draws vertical lines on 1" x 12" paper strip. (Newsprint to protect child's desk.)
4. Child cuts lined strip into design pieces and tongue.
5. Child makes selection from scrap box.
6. Set up for gluing.
7. Lay spiral into a flat circle, then glue design pieces onto Snake.
8. Clean up (except for crayons).
9. Child adds drawings to snake.

Note: Children may create independent ideas with these materials.

Children's Ideas

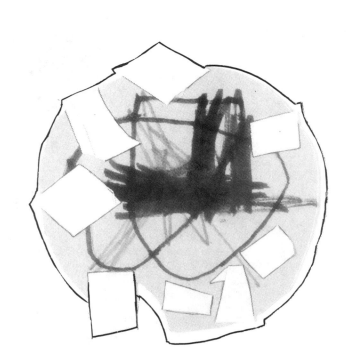

Cheerleader skirt

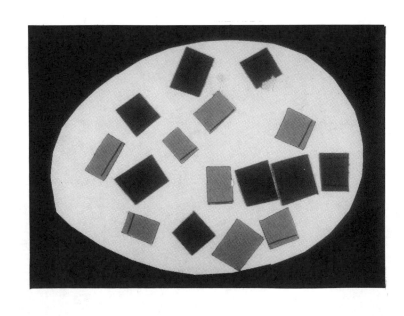

Children's Ideas

135

Teacher Ideas

1. Child draws own large scribble design; then fills in open spaces with snipped paper.
2. Child draws lines on strip, snips "blocks," glues "blocks" onto background material to make block buildings.
3. See Reciprocal Tearing Activities.
4. See Free Cutting - Snipping Activities.

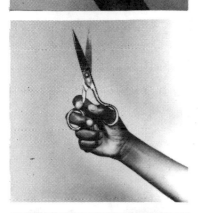

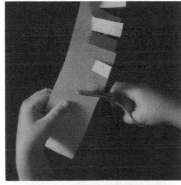

Fringe-Line

I. Instructions

A. Skill

Stopping the scissor action at the end of a line.

B. Language

fringe   long line   strip   end of the line

C. Materials

1. Paper Strips
   Length does not matter.
   Width about one inch longer than the scissors blade.
2. Pencil, Marker or Crayon.
3. The child draws bold lines half way across the width of the paper at intervals about one inch apart. (Again the fingers can help with spacing. Also a crease or line down the middle of the paper may be necessary as a starting point for drawing the lines.) **137**
4. Newsprint to protect the child's desk from drawing marks.

D. Procedure

NOTE: Refer to photos for free cutting.

1. Relaxed cutting position.
2. One cut along the lines, beginning with the one closest to the scissors hand. (Again check to be sure the line is inside the scissors blade when the child is using scissors appropriate for his handness.)
3. Scissors blades are completely opened.
4. At the point where the paper-holding hand needs to move, the scissors blades should hold the paper.
5. Scissors DO NOT close (essential skill.)

II. Problems and Solutions

A. Cannot cut along an extended line.

1. Make the visual checks as in Skill 1, Snip-Line.
2. Provide activities with lines as in Skill 1, Snip-Line.
3. Return to free cutting a fringe.

B. Cannot stop at the end of the line.

1. Visual checks as in "A."
2. Review the Problems and Solution of free cutting a fringe.
3. Provide gross and fine motor activities which require stopping at the end of a line.
4. Consider the placement of the line along the scissors blade. Left-handed children using right-handed scissors have the difficult task of cutting along a line behind the scissors blade. Try left-handed scissors for these children.

Woven Headband

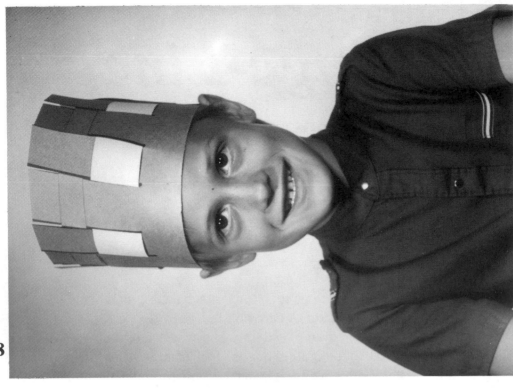

Supplies

Scissors
Glue
Paper Towels
Pencils/Crayons
Newsprint
Straight Edge
Stapler
Scrap Box

Teacher-Prepared Materials

Paper Rectangle, 4" x 24" (Strips)
Paper Rectangle, 6" x 24"
draw a 24" line down the middle of
the strip (Child's name on back.)

Procedure

1. Small group discussion.
a. Talk about and demonstrate
cutting a lined fringe in a full
stroke without closing
the scissors completely.
b. Talk about and demonstrate
using a straight edge (or the
line may be drawn freehand.)

NOTE: Straight Edge should be longer
than line to be drawn. Talk about and
demonstrate drawing the line starting
from the middle line to the edge of the
6" x 24" paper strip.

d. Pass out scissors, newsprint,
straight edge and Teacher-Prepared Materials.

e. Let children tell you about:
   1. drawing the lines;
   2. cutting the fringe;
   3. making this Headband.
*2. Child draws perpendicular
line from the middle line to the
edge of the 6" x 24" strip. (Use
finger, a straight edge or sim-
ply draw the lines freehand. Put
down newsprint to protect
child's desk).*
3. Child cuts:
   a. lined 6" x 24" fringe;
   b. unlined 4" x 24" into 24"
   long strips.
4. Child weaves strips into

fringed strip (*Weaving maybe
irregular, use the childs judgement for how the weave should
look*).
*5. Set up for gluing; glue ran-
dom spots in the weaving to hold
the strips in place.*
6. Child adds items from the

scrap box to his Headband.
7. Clean up.
*8. Teacher measures Headband
to fit child's head and staples
Headband.*

Note: Children may create independent ideas with these materials.

Baby Bird In Nest

Supplies

Scissors
Glue
Paper Towels
Pencils/Crayons
Newsprint
Straight Edge
Scrap Box

Teacher-Prepared Materials

Paper Strip, 9" x 3"
  Draw 9" line down middle of strip (Nest)
Paper Square, 3" x 3" (Head)
Paper Square, 4" x 4" (Body)
Paper Rectangle, 2" x 4" (Wing & Tail)
Paper Rectangle, 1" x 2" (Beak)
Small scrap for Eye
Background Paper, 9" x 12" (Child's name on back.)

Procedure

1. Small group discussion.
a. Talk about baby birds; have pictures.
b. Talk about each piece of paper and demonstrate what part of the project it could become.
c. Pass out scissors, newsprint and Teacher-Prepared Materials.
d. Talk about and demonstrate drawing the lines on the 9" x 3" nest.
e. Let children tell you:
1. about drawing the lines;
2. how they will make the Baby Bird in Nest;
3. their own ideas.

2. Child draws vertical lines from middle line to edge on 9" x 3" strip; with straight edge finger or free hand. (Newsprint to protect child's desk.)

3. Child cuts:
a. lined 9" x 3" strip into nest;
b. 3" x 3" into circle for head;
c. 4" x 4" into circle for body;
d. 2" x 4" diagonally into triangles for wing and tail; fringe wing and tail;
e. 1" x 2" into triangles for beak.
f. scrap into eye.

4. Child lays out Baby Bird in Nest.
5. Child adds her additional items to collage.
6. Set up for gluing; glue:
a. crumple nest onto 9" x 12";
b. body into nest;
c. head onto body;
d. wing and tail onto body;
e. beak and eye onto head.
7. Clean up.

Note: Children may create independent ideas with these materials.

139

Giraffe

Supplies

Scissors
Glue
Paper Towels
Pencils/Crayons/Markers
Newsprint
Straight Edge
Scrap Box

Procedure

1. Small group discussion.
a. Talk about Giraffes; show pictures/models.
b. Talk about how to cut each piece of paper and demonstrate what part of the project it could become.
c. Pass out scissors, newsprint and Teacher-Prepared Materials.
d. Children place newsprint on their desks (to protect their desks while they are marking on the paper strips).
e. Let children tell you how to make their Giraffes.

Teacher-Prepared Materials

Paper Strip, 1" x 9"
Draw 9" line down middle of strip (Mane)
Paper Strip, tapered 8" long;

1" across top
5" across bottom (Body)

(Cut 6" x 8" on the diagonal get 2 bodies)
(Child's name on back.)

Paper Strip, 1" x 6" (Head and Legs)
Paper Strip, 1" x 12" (Spots and Horns)

2. Child draws vertical lines from the middle line to the edge of the 1" x 9" mane.
3. Child cuts:
a. lined strip into mane;
b. 1" x 6" strip, snip off head; then fold remaining length in half; snip on the fold, then cut each piece into 2 legs;
c. 1" x 12" strip, snip off 2 pieces horns, then snip into squares and cutting squares into circles for spots.
4. Child lays out Giraffe.
5. Set up for gluing; glue:
a. mane to body;
b. head to body;
c. horns to head;
d. spots to body;
e. legs to body;
f. any additional items the child chooses.

6. Child helps to clean up work area (except for pencils/crayons/markers).

7. Child draws eyes, nostrils, mouth and ears.

Note: Children may create independent ideas with these materials.

Alligator

Supplies

Scissors
Glue
Paper Towels
Pencils/Crayons/Markers
Newsprint
Scrap Box

Teacher-Prepared Materials

2 Paper Strips, 2" x 6" (Mouth)
Paper Strip, 5" x 3" (Eye Backs)
Paper Strip, 2" x 4" (Eyes)
Paper Rectangle, 5" x 6" (Tail)
Paper Strip, 1" x 4" (Bumps for Tail)
Background Paper, 9" x 12"
(Child's name on back.)

Procedure

1. Small group discussion.
a. Talk about Alligators; have pictures/models.
b. Talk about and demonstrate each piece of paper and what part of the project it could become.
c. Talk about and demonstrate drawing an angled line.
d. Pass out scissors, newsprint and Teacher-Prepared Materials.
e. Let children tell you how to:
  1. draw an angled line;
  2. make their Alligators;
  3. let children tell you what they will make.

2. Child draws:
a. angled lines for teeth along the two 2" x 6" paper strips (mouth);
b. angled lines along the 1" x 4" paper strip (bumps for tail).

3. Child cuts:
a. angled lines on 2" x 6" strip into teeth; round corners of strip for mouth;
b. angled lines on 1" x 4" strip into bumps for tail;
c. 5" x 3" into 2 1/2" x 3" rectangle into semicircles for eye backs;
d. use c. scraps to cut semi-circle nostrils;
e. 2" x 4" into 2" x 2" squares, rounding corners into circles for eyes;
f. 5" x 6" into triangle for tail;
g. use f. scraps to cut 2 circles for eye centers.

4. Child lays out Alligator.

5. Child adds additional items to her alligator as she pleases.

6. Set up for gluing; glue:
a. mouth strips to 9" x 12" background;
b. tail to mouth;
c. eye backs, eyes, eye centers;
d. bumps down tail;
e. nostrils to mouth.

7. Child helps to clean up work area (except for pencils/crayons/markers.)

Bugs In The Grass

Supplies

Scissors
Glue
Paper Towels
Pencils/Crayons/Markers
Newsprint
Scrap Box

Teacher-Prepared Materials

4 Paper Rectangles, 2" x 12" (Grass)
Paper Rectangle, 1" x 12" (Bug Bodies)
Odd Scraps from other projects may be used to
  cut bug bodies and legs
Paper Rectangle, 2" x 12" (Bug Legs)
Paper Rectangle, 2" x 6" (Caterpillar)
Background Paper, 12" x 18"
  (Child's name on back.)

Procedure

1. Small group discussion.

a. Talk about bugs; have pictures.

b. Talk about each piece of paper and demonstrate what part of the project it could become.

c. Pass out scissors, newsprint and Teacher-Prepared Materials.

d. Let children tell you:
   1. how to make their Bugs in the Grass;
   2. what they will make.

2. Child draws:

a. vertical line along one 12" edge of the 4, 2" x 12" rect-

angles for grass;

b. vertical lines along each 6" edge of the 2" x 6" rectangle for the caterpillar legs (place newsprint on child's desk under the paper strips).

3. Child cuts:

a. lines on the 4, 2" x 12" rectangles for grass;

b. lines on the 2" x 12" rectangle for caterpillar legs;

c. 1" x 12" into smaller pieces (circles and ovals for bug bodies);

d. 2" x 12" into small strips for bugs' legs and antennae.

4. Child lays out Bugs in the Grass.

5. Child adds additional items to collage.

6. Set up for gluing; glue:
   a. legs and antennae to bugs;
   b. grass to background paper;
   c. bugs and caterpillar to grass

and background paper.

7. Child helps to clean up work area.

Note: Children may create independent ideas with these materials.

Tropical Rain Forest

Supplies

Scissors
Glue
Paper Towels
Pencils/Crayons/Markers
Newsprint
36" Yarn
Scrap Box

Teacher-Prepared Materials

Paper Rectangle, 6" x 9" (Tree Trunks)
Paper Rectangle, 6" x 9" (Palm Fronds)
Paper Strip, 3" x 9" (Ferns)
Background Paper, 9" x 12" (Child's name on back.)

Procedure

1. Small group discussion.
a. Talk about the tropical rain forest; have pictures.
b. Talk about how to cut each piece of paper and demonstrate what it could become.
c. Pass out scissors, newsprint and your Teacher-Prepared Materials.
d. Let children tell you how to make their Tropical Rain Forests.
e. Let children tell you what they will make.

2. Child cuts and draws:
a. cut 6" x 9" into 3 tree trunks approximately 6" x 3", then draw lines to fringe (this fringe will be the base for gluing the tree onto the background piece);
  1. draw vertical lines about 2/3" long along the 6" length for 3" tall trees;
  2. draw vertical lines about 2/3" long along the 3" length for 6" tall trees (use newsprint to protect desk);
b. cut lined tree trunks;

c. cut 6" x 9" strips for palm fronds, fringe strips (drawing lines to fringe is optional);
d. cut 3" x 9" into 3" strips for ferns, fringe strips (drawing lines to fringe is optional);
e. cut the yarn into smaller lengths.

3. Child plans layout for Tropical Rain Forest.

4. Child adds additional items to collage.

5. Set up for gluing; glue:
a. tree trunks into a tube, then spread out fringed end and glue to 9" x 12" background paper;
b. palm fronds onto tree trunks;
c. ferns onto background paper;
d. small scraps onto yarn (for leaves);
e. yarn vines onto trees.

6. Child helps to clean up work area.

Note: Children may create independent ideas with these materials.

143

Children's Ideas

Children's Ideas

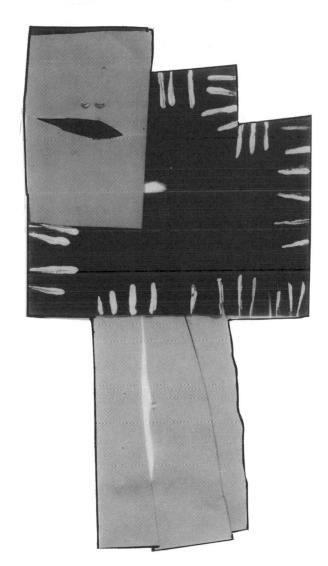

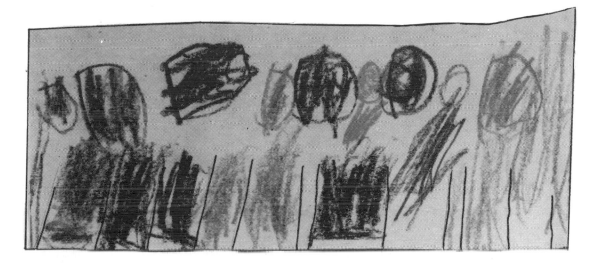

Teacher Ideas

1. Take paper pieces from your scrap box, draw fringe lines and cut. Your children will join you to make all kinds of floppy things.
2. Show your children how to cut a drawn line on one paper, then cut a drawn line on another paper and fit them together.
3. See Free Cutting Fringe ideas.

146

Skill Three

Strip-Line

I. Instructions

A. Skill
1. Move scissors following a line.
2. Guide the lined paper into the scissors.

B. Language

ruler	across	start	finish
move	far apart	close	together
wide	narrow	parallel	

C. Short-Line
1. Materials
   a. Paper Squares
      not larger than 6" x 6"
      not smaller than 4" x 4"

   b. Pencils, Markers or Crayons.
   c. Ruler/Straight Edge (We will not measure, so any flat stick can be used as a guide. The numbers are unimportant.)
   d. The ruler/straight edge or any line guide is placed perpendicular to the body. The child draws lines down the square towards the body. Start at the left side of the square for a right-handed child and the right side of the square for a left-handed child. The distance between the lines is unimportant at this time. Talk with the children about the distance between the lines. Help them understand that lines which are far apart will be wide strips, and lines that are close together will be narrow strips. Also talk about the importance of lines being parallel. The line guide should extend beyond the edges of both sides of the square to ensure success.
   e. Newsprint to protect the child's desk from drawing marks.
2. Procedure
NOTE: Photos - free cutting.
   a. Relaxed cutting posture.
   b. Hold the strip so that the bold lines are at about an 80-degree angle to the body.
   c. The paper-holding hand should be on the side parallel to the lines.
   d. Cutting should begin on the side farthest from the holding hand and at the bottom of the paper.
   e. Line is inside the scissors blade, next to the body (except when using right-handed scissors in the left hand).

f. Scissors blades are completely opened.

g. The holding hand moves the paper into a cutting position.

h. When the hands are about parallel, the cutting stops. The paper is held between the scissors blades, and the paper-holding hand moves away from the body and catches the paper at a place nearer the top of the paper. Cutting begins again. (When using a smaller square, the child may not need to move the holding hand.)

i. A natural rhythm of cut, slip, cut, slip, while the paper-holding hand moves toward the top of the paper, is developed.

D. Long-Line
  1. Materials
    a. Paper rectangles .
      6" to 8" long
      4" to 6" wide
    b. Pencil, Crayon, Marker.
    c. Ruler
    d. Draw lines as with the square. The child will find it easier if the line guide laps over both edges of the rectangle.
    e. Newsprint to protect the child's desk from drawing marks.
  2. Procedure
    a. Relaxed cutting position.
    b. Proceed as with the square.
    c. When the rectangle is long enough, the paper-holding hand should naturally move to the top of the paper.
    d. A left-handed child using right-handed scissors may need help with line placement next to the scissors blade.

II. Problems and Solutions

A. Review "Strip" problems of free cutting.

B. Continue to be aware of problems that visual development may contribute.

C. Continue to offer left-handed children left-handed scissors.

D. Child does not cross his mid-line when drawing the line.

(The child will keep the paper and ruler on the dominant side of his body while drawing the lines.)

  1. Help the child to place the paper directly in front of him and help him draw the line.
  2. Provide activities which require the child to cross his mid-line.
  3. Remember the placement of the glue on his non-dominant side requires him to cross his mid-line.

148

Animal And People Headband

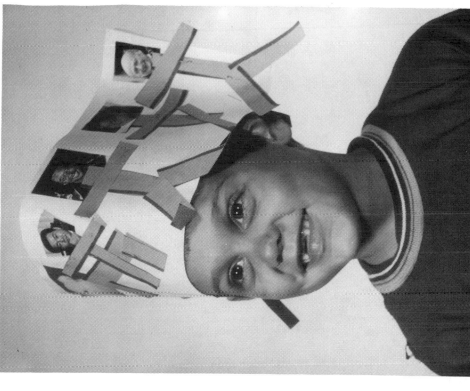

Supplies

Scissors
Glue
Paper Towels
Newsprint
Magazine
Straight Edge
Scrap Box

Teacher-Prepared Materials

Paper Rectangle, 3" x 18" for Stick People
Paper Strip, 6" x 24"
(Child's name on back.)

Procedure

1. Small group discussion.

a. Talk about people; look at children in the room and talk about body parts.

b. Talk about animals; have models; talk about body parts.

c. Talk about and demonstrate drawing lines across the 3" x 18" paper.

d. Talk about spacing lines for wide and narrow pieces.

e. Talk about placing the line on the inside of the scissors blade for cutting.

f. Talk about what could be used from the scrap box;

g. Pass out scissors, newsprint, straight edge, magazines and Teacher-Prepared Materials.

h. Let children tell you about:
 1. using the straight edge;
 2. spacing the lines;
 3. placing the line on the inside of the scissors blade;
 4. how to make their People Headband.

2. Child finds 6 to 8 heads of people and animals in magazine and cuts them out or any other items she may want to put on the Headband. (Then pick up the magazines to get them out of the way.)

3. Child draws vertical lines along the 3" x 18" rectangle using finger for spacer. Drawing guide is optional. (Newsprint under the 3" x 18" rectangle before drawing the line. This allows the child to draw off

of the rectangle onto the newsprint without marking up the desk.)

4. Child cuts along lines on 3" x 18" rectangle to make body parts.

5. Child lays out people and animals on headband.

6. Set up for gluing; glue each complete figure one by one, starting with the head.

7. Clean up.

8. Add drawings to Headband.

9. Child measures Headband to fit head and staples Headband.

Note: Children may create independent ideas with these materials.

Game Stadium

Supplies

Scissors
Glue
Paper Towels
Crayons/Pencils/Marker
Newsprint
Cardboard/Wooden Straight Edge
Scrap Box

Teacher-Prepared Materials

2 Paper Squares, 3" x 3"
Paper Rectangle, 3" x 8"
Background Paper, 9" x 12"
(Child's name on back.)

Procedure

1. Small group discussion.

a. Talk about game stadiums and what kind of things happen in them; have pictures; talk about the one in your town and your children's experiences there.

b. Talk about each piece of paper and demonstrate what it could become.

c. Talk about using the straight edge to draw lines.

d. Pass out scissors, newsprint,

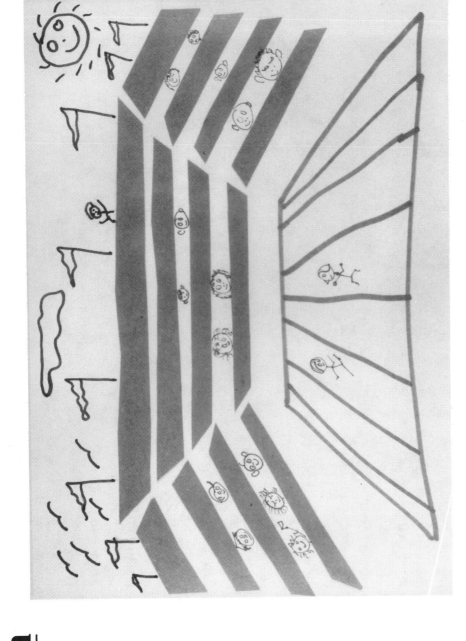

straight edge and Teacher Prepared Materials.

e. Let children tell you about:

1. using the straight edge;
2. how to make their Game Stadium;
3. what they will add from the scrap box;
4. what to do with the newsprint.

2. Child uses the straight edge to draw:

a. 3" lines across 3" x 3" square;
b. 8" lines across 3" x 8" rectangle.

3. Child cuts:

a. 3" x 3" into end zone seats;
b. 3" x 8" into sideline seats.

4. Lays out Game Stadium.

5. Set up for gluing; glue:

a. sidelines in center of background paper;
b. end zone to background paper.

6. Clean up.

7. Child adds drawings to project.

Note: Children may create independent ideas with these materials.

Lion In A Cage

Supplies

Scissors
Glue
Paper Towels
Crayons/Pencils/Marker
Newsprint
Straight Edge
Scrap Box

Teacher-Prepared Materials

Paper Rectangle, 6" x 12" (Cage)
Paper Rectangle, 2" x 4" (Lion's Body)
Paper Square, 4" x 4" (Lion's Head)
Paper Square, 2" x 2" (Lion's Legs and Tail)
Background Paper, 9" x 12"
(Child's name on back.)

Procedure

1. Small group discussion.
  a. Talk about zoos and cir-
  cuses and animals in cages;
  have pictures.
  b. Talk about lions; have pictures.
  c. Talk about each piece of
  paper and demonstrate what
  it could become.
  d. Pass out scissors, newsprint, straight edge and

Teacher Prepared Materials.
  e. Let children tell you:
  1. how to make their Lion in
  a Cage;
  2. what they will make;
  3. what to do with their
  newsprint.
*2. Child draws 6" vertical lines
  across 6" x 12" rectangle using
  the straight edge.*
3. Child cuts:
  a. 6" x 12" into strips;
  b. 2" x 4" into lion's body;
  c. 4" x 4" into circle for head;
  fringe for mane;
  d. 2" x 2" into 4 legs and tail;
  e. scraps into eyes, nose and
  mouth.
4. Child lays out Lion in a Cage.
5. Set up for gluing; glue:
  a. lion's body in center of back

ground paper;
  b. lion's legs and tail to body;
  c. paper strips into a cage
  around the lion's body;
  d. head to body on top of cage;
  e. eyes, nose, mouth to head;
  f. items from scrap box.
6. Clean up.

Note: Children may create independent ideas with these materials.

151

Castle

Supplies

Scissors
Glue
Paper Towels
Pencils/Crayons
Newsprint
Straight Edge
Toothpicks
Cellophane Tape
Scrap Box

Teacher-Prepared Materials

Paper Rectangle, 9" x 12" (4 Towers)
Paper Rectangle, 4" x 10" (2 Towers)
Paper Rectangle, 1" x 18"
  (Windows and Doors)
Paper Square, 5" x 5" (Roof)
Paper Strip, 4" x 18" (Wall)
  (Draw 18" line down the middle of the strip)
Scraps (Flags)

Procedure

1. Small group discussion.
  a. Talk about castles; have pictures, models.
  b. Talk about each piece of paper and demonstrate what part of the Castle it could become.
  c. Talk about drawing lines across the 9" x 12" and 4" x 10" rectangle. (You may want to pre-mark a starting point.)
  d. Pass out scissors, newsprint, straight edge, and Teacher Prepared Materials.
  e. Let children tell you about:
    1. drawing lines on a rectangle;
    2. how to make their Castle.

2. Using a straight edge, the child draws:
  a. one 10" vertical line down the middle of the10" x 4" rectangle (you may want to pre-mark a starting point);
  b. three 9" vertical lines across the 9" x 12" rectangle (pre-mark starting points).

3. Child cuts:
  a. 4" x 10" into 2" x 10" for 2 buildings;
  b. 9" x 12" into 3" x 9" for 4 buildings;
  c. 1" x 18" into smaller pieces for doors and windows;
  d. scraps into flags;
  e. 4" x 18" into 2" x 18" for wall (draw boulders on the wall if desired);
  f. 5" x 5" square into circle; cut slot to the center of the circle;
  g. items from scrap box.

4. Set up for gluing; glue:
  a. 3" x 9" and 2" x 10" strips into circular buildings;
  b. windows and doors onto buildings;
  c. flags onto toothpicks;
  d. 2" x 18" strips together, then into circle for wall;
  e. circle into cone for roof.

5. Lay out Castle.

6. Cut and glue:
  a. cut 1/2" slots in the top of the bottom buildings, slip second story buildings into slot and glue;
  b. cut 1/2" slots in the top of the second story buildings, slip third story building into slot and glue;
  c. glue roof to third story building;
  d. glue some of the buildings to the wall;
  e. tape flags to buildings.

7. Clean up.

Note: Children may create independent ideas with these materials.

Placemat

Supplies

Scissors
Glue
Paper Towels
Newsprint
Straight Edge

Teacher-Prepared Materials

Paper Rectangle, (Color One) 9" x 12"
Paper Rectangle, (Color Two) 6" x 9"
Paper Rectangle, (Color Three) 6" x 9"

Procedure

1. Small group discussion.
a. Talk about placemats.
b. Talk about and demonstrate weaving.
c. Talk about each piece of paper and demonstrate what it will become.
d. Talk about and demonstrate using a straight edge to draw long lines.
e. Pass out scissors, newsprint, straight edge and Teacher-Prepared Materials.

2. Child draws:
a. 12" horizontal lines across the 9" x 12" rectangle;
b. 9" vertical lines down the 6" x 9" rectangle.

3. Child cuts:
a. 9" x 12" rectangle into strips;
b. 6" x 9" rectangle into strips.

4. Child glues:
a. start with one of the strips from the 9" x 12" rectangle (color one);
b. glue color two strip perpendicular to color one strip;
c. glue color three onto color one next to color two;
d. glue color two next to color three;
e. glue color three next to color two;
f. etc.; until all color two and color three strips are glued to color one;

5. Child weaves:
a. take color one strip, put it on top of color two; under color three; top of color two; under color three; etc.;
b. take color one strip; put it under color two; top of color three; under color two; top of color three; etc.;
c. continue until all strips are woven;
d. use child's judgement as to the "correctness" of the weave of the placemat. Value his work in the project rather than how exactly the strips are woven;
e. glue end pieces of the Placemat together.

6. Clean up.

Note: Children may create independent ideas with these materials.

153

Balloon and Basket

Supplies

Scissors
Glue
Paper Towels
Pencils/Crayons/Markers
Newsprint
Straight Edge

Teacher-Prepared Materials

Paper Rectangle, 3" x 4" - Color One - (Basket)
Paper Rectangle, 2" x 3" - Color Two - (Basket)
Paper Rectangle, 2" x 3" - Color Three - (Basket)
Paper Square, 6" x 6" (Balloon)
Background Paper, 9" x 12" (Child's name on back.)

Procedure

1. Small group discussion.
a. Talk about hot air balloons; have pictures.
b. Talk about each piece of paper and demonstrate what it could become.
c. Talk about drawing the lines across the rectangles.
d. Pass out scissors, newspaper, straight edge and Teacher-Prepared Materials.
e. Let children tell you about:
 1. drawing lines across the rectangles;
 2. how to weave;
 3. how to make a Balloon and Basket.

2. Child draws:
a. 3" vertical lines across the 3" x 4" rectangle;
b. 3" vertical lines across the 3" x 2" rectangles.

3. Child cuts:
a. 3" x 4" rectangle into strips for basket;
b. 3" x 2" rectangles into strips for basket;
c. 6" x 6" square into circle for balloon.

4. Child weaves basket:
a. start with one of the strips from the 3" x 4" rectangle (color one);
b. glue color two strip perpendicular to color one;
c. glue color three onto color one next to color two;
d. glue color two onto color one next to color three;
e. glue color three onto color one next to color two;
f. etc. until all color two and three strips are glued onto color one; NOTE: You may let the children draw a design on the balloon to give the glue some drying time.
g. take color one strip; put it on top of color two; under color three; top of color two; under color three; etc.;
h. take color one strip; put it under color two; over color three; under color two; over color three; etc.;
i. continue until all strips are woven (child may have strips left over);
j. glue end pieces of the basket together.

5. Child lays out basket, balloon and string.

6. Child glues:
a. basket to background piece;
b. balloon to background piece;
c. string/yarn between basket and balloon.

7. Clean up.

8. Child adds drawings to project.

Note: Children may create independent ideas with these materials.

Children's Ideas

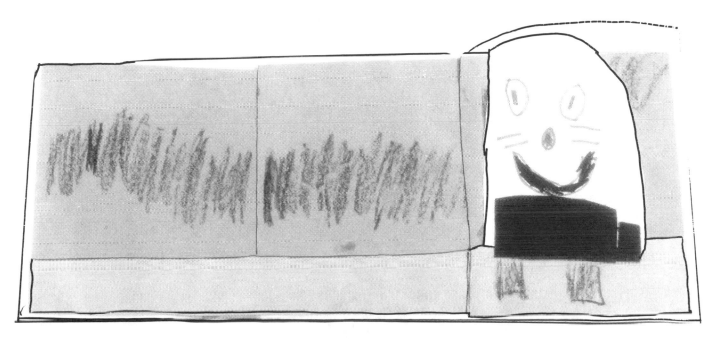

Children's Ideas

Teacher Ideas

1. Put out an assortment of paper and cloth to cut.
2. Continue to believe in your children's eagerness to cut independent creations.
3. Your children may still choose to cut and throw away, so provide plenty of scrap paper.

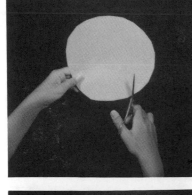

Skill Four

Sides And Angles-Line

NOTE: These skills are combined because the paper manipulation skills of cutting sides and angles were learned during free cutting.

I. Instructions

NOTE: Before and in conjunction with this step, the child should have many experiences with angle lined shapes: walking, drawing, crawling, sorting, finding, building, and talking about squares, rectangles, triangles, and other angled shapes. Also, give the child instruction and practice time with using angled templates, before and during this skill.

A. Skill

  1. Positioning a lined angle in relation to the scissors blade.

  2. Cutting a drawn corner.

B. Language

template	inside	around
clipboard	push	apart
ruler	line	guide

C. Paper Square

  1. Materials

    a. Paper square.

      Not larger than 8" x 8"

      Not smaller than 6" x 6"

    b. Pencils, Crayons, Markers.

    c. Square template no larger than the size of the paper square.

NOTE: A template is a cut-out pattern. Use a template with the square pattern cut out inside of a piece of wood, cardboard, or plastic. Drawing inside of the cut out pattern rather than drawing around the outside of the pattern is an easier task for the child. Packing materials often have circles or squares cut into cardboard. These make good templates. (Make sure the materials are non-toxic.) Templates are also available commercially, or you can make your own.

    d. Clipboard.

NOTE: A clipboard will hold the template and the paper steady while the child draws the pattern inside.

e. Line Guide, Ruler or Straight Edge - Have the child: draw a line all the way across the paper; turn the paper; draw another line across the paper; continue 2 more times. When finished, there will be a drawn square. Children cannot at this level use a ruler to connect lines to draw a square. Thus we use this method of drawing 4 lines which "become a square."

f. Also encourage children to draw free-hand squares almost the size of the paper.

2. Procedure

NOTE: Photos for Free Cutting.

a. Relaxed cutting posture.

b. Begin cutting at the bottom of the paper square at the line.

c. Cut beside the line of the drawn square nearest the cutting hand.

Note: For squares drawn free-hand, cutting begins at the bottom of the paper; cut towards the drawn side nearest the scissors hand.

d. Cut along the line, keeping the line inside of the scissors blade.

e. Use the full length of the scissors blade for cutting.

f. Cut past the drawn square corner, about a quarter of an inch, as was done in free cutting.

g. Move the paper-holding hand towards the body. Catch the paper and turn so that the newly cut edge will be parallel to the body.

h. Move scissors into cutting position and cut to the middle of the new side.

i. Turn paper to easily snip off the excess paper.

j. Continue to cut the side, again stopping about a quarter of an inch past the drawn square corner.

k. Proceed as in b through h, until a square is cut.

l. Although the full length of the blade is used, scissors are not to close completely while cutting the straight edges (essential skill).

m. Scissors may close on final snip and when separating the square from excess paper.

n. Verbally label the shape as square, edges as straight edges, and corners as corners and angles.

159

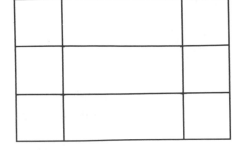

D. Paper Rectangle
1. Materials
   a. Paper rectangle.
      not larger than 6" x 8"
      not smaller than 4" x 6"
   b. Pencils, Markers, Crayons.
   c. Rectangle template no larger than the size of the paper rectangle.
   d. Clipboard.
   e. Ruler/Straight Edge - Line Guide (Draw rectangle as C. Paper Square, e. Line Guide, Ruler or Straight Edge.)
   f. Free-hand drawn rectangles almost the size of the paper rectangle.
2. Procedure
   a. Relaxed cutting position.
   b. Hold paper so that the longest side of the drawn rectangle nearest the cutting hand is cut first.
   c. Follow the directions to cut a square.
   d. Label new shapes as rectangles.

160

E. Paper Triangle
1. Materials
   a. Paper square or rectangle.
      not larger than 8" x 8"
      not smaller than 4" x 4"
   b. Pencils, Markers, Crayons.
   c. Triangle template (equilateral, isosceles, and/or scalene) not larger than the size of the paper square or rectangle.
   d. Clipboard.
   e. Ruler/Straight Edge - Line Guide (use pre-cut triangle and draw lines as in C. Paper Square, e. Line Guide, Ruler or Straight Edge.)
   f. Paper triangle for free-hand drawn triangles almost the size of the paper.
2. Procedure
   a. Relaxed cutting position.
   b. Follow square directions to cut triangles. Label new shapes as triangles.

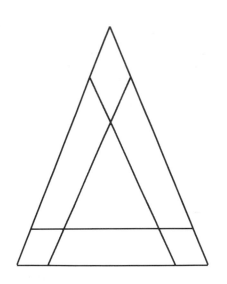

II. Problems and Solutions

A. Review sides and angles free cutting.

B. Difficulty following the angled lines:

1. Continue body involvement with lined angled shapes.
2. Try giving the child pieces of paper with only one drawn 90 degree corner, then two, and then three, and finally four.
3. Continue to make visual checks.
4. Offer left-handed children left-handed scissors.
5. Use a paper triangle to draw the line triangle.

Collage Headband

Supplies

Scissors
Glue
Paper Towels
Newsprint
Pencils/Crayons/Marker
Straight Edge
Scrap Box

Teacher-Prepared Materials

6 Paper Rectangles, 5 1/2" x 6"
Paper Strip, 6" x 24"
(Child's name on back.)

Procedure

1. Small group discussion.
a. Talk about and demonstrate drawing a rectangle with 4 lines and a straight edge.
b. Talk about and demonstrate cutting a drawn rectangle.
c. Pass out scissors, newsprint, straight edge and Teacher-Prepared Materials.
d. Let children tell you about:
  1. drawing a rectangle with a straight edge;
  2. cutting a drawn rectangle;
  3. how to make their Headband;
  4. what they will make.

2. Child draws on 5 1/2" x 6" rectangle:
a. place straight edge along bottom edge of rectangle;
b. draw a line across 6" side;
c. turn rectangle;
d. draw a line across 5 1/2" side;
e. turn rectangle;
f. draw a line across 6" side,
g. turn rectangle;
h. draw a line across 5 1/2" side.

3. Child cuts:
a. lined 5 1/2" x 6" rectangles into drawn rectangles;
b. scraps into pieces which please him.

4. Lay out Collage Headband.
5. Set up for gluing; glue pieces on Headband.
6. Child helps to clean up work area.

7. *Measure Headband to fit child's head, and staple.*

Note: Children may create independent ideas with these materials.

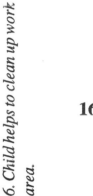

161

Cruise Ship

Supplies

Scissors
Glue
Paper Towels
Pencils/Crayons/Markers
Newsprint
Straight Edge
Scrap Box

Teacher-Prepared Materials

Paper Rectangle, 4" x 9" (Boat)
Paper Strip, 1/2" x 5" (Portholes)
Paper Strip, 1" x 9" (Waves)
Background Paper, 9" x 12" (Child's name on back.)

Procedure

1. Small group discussion.
   a. Talk about Cruise Ships;
show pictures and models.
   b. Talk about and demonstrate how the strips need to be
cut shorter as they go to the
top of the Cruise Ship.
   c. Talk about and demonstrate drawing angled lines on
the strips to get pointed waves.
   d. Pass out scissors, newsprint, straight edge and

Teacher-Prepared Materials.
   e. Let children tell you about:
   1. drawing the angled lines;
   2. how to make their Cruise
Ships;
   3. what they will make.
*2. Child draws angled lines on
1" x 9" paper strips using the
straight edge.*
3. Child cuts:
   a. angled lines on 1" x 9"
into waves;
   b. 4" x 9" into four strips:
   1. 1" x 9" into Cruise Ship
decks;
   2. scraps into smoke stacks.
   c. 1/2" x 5" into portholes.
*4. Child lays out Cruise Ship
with items from scrap box.*
5. Set up for gluing; and glue:
   a. longest strip for hull;
   b. build decks by length;
   c. portholes on Cruise Ship;
   d. waves onto background
pieces;

*6. Child helps to clean up (ex-
cept for pencils/crayons/mark-
ers).*
*7. Child adds drawings to pic-
ture.*

Note: Children may create independent projects with these materials,
using their own ideas.

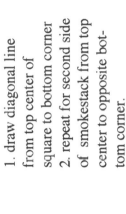

Train

Supplies

Scissors
Glue
Pencils/Crayons/Markers
Newsprint
Straight Edge
Paper Towels
Scrap Box

Teacher-Prepared Materials

Paper Rectangle, 5" x 12" (engine)
Paper Rectangle, 4" x 5" (cab)
Paper Rectangle, 3" x 4" (cab window)
Paper Rectangle, 3" x 4" (cattle catcher)
Paper Square, 2" x 2" (smokestack)
Paper Rectangle, 2" x 10" (wheels)
Background Paper, 9" x 12"
(Child's name on back.)

Procedure

1. Small group discussion.
a. Talk about trains; have pictures and models.
b. Talk about and demonstrate how to draw the lines to cut the engine, cab, cab window, cattle catcher and smokestack.
c. Let children tell you about:
  1. using the straight edge to draw the engine, cab, cab window, cattle catcher and smokestack;
  2. how to make their Trains;
  3. what they will make.

2. Child draws:
a. cab window on 3" x 4" :
  1. draw 4" line across the bottom of the rectangle;
  2. draw 3" line down the side of the rectangle;
  3. repeat 3" line down the other side;
  4. Draw 4" line across the top of the rectangle.
b. cab on 4" x 5":
follow the same process of drawing the rectangle line by line;
c. engine on 5" x 12" as in a. and b.;
d. cattle catcher on 3" x 4":
  1. draw one diagonal line across the rectangle
e. smokestack on 2" x 2"

1. draw diagonal line from top center of square to bottom corner
2. repeat for second side of smokestack from top center to opposite bottom corner.

3. Child cuts:
a. lines on 3" x 4" into drawn rectangle for cab window;
b. lines on 4" x 5" into drawn rectangle for cab
c. lines on 5" x 12" into drawn rectangle for engine
d. line on 3" x 4" into drawn triangle for cattle catcher
e. lines on 2" x 2" into drawn triangle for smokestack;
f. 2" x 10" fold in half :
  1. cut on fold to 2" x 5";
  2. fold 2" x 5";
  3. cut on fold (you now have 4 pieces);
  4. cut into circles for wheels.
g. using scraps cut:
  1. bell;
  2. driver bar

4. Set up for gluing; glue:
a. engine on background paper;
b. cab to engine;
c. window to cab;
d. cattle catcher to engine;
e. bell and smokestack to engine;
f. wheels to engine;
g. driver bar to engine.

5. Child helps to clean up work area.
Note: Children may create independent ideas with these materials.

Ice Cream Treats

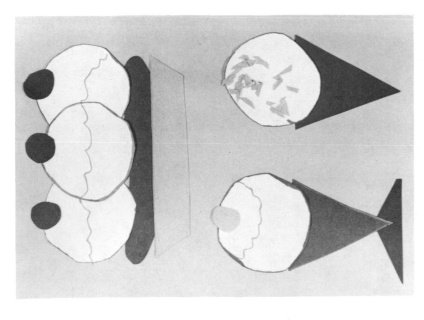

Supplies

Scissors
Glue
Paper Towels
Pencils/Crayons/Markers
Newsprint
Straight Edge

Teacher-Prepared Materials

2 Paper Squares, 3" x 3" (Cone, Sundae Dish)
Paper Rectangles, 6" x 2" (Banana Split Dish)
Paper Rectangle, 1" x 6" (Banana)
5 Paper Squares, 3" x 3" (Ice Cream Scoops)
Background Paper, 9" x 12"
   (Child's name on back.)

Procedure

1. Small group discussion.

a. Talk about ice cream; where to get it; flavors; ways to eat it; "have samples!";

b. Talk about and demonstrate how to draw cone, sundae dish and banana split dish;

c. Pass out scissors, newsprint, straight edge and Teacher-Prepared materials;

d. Let children tell you about:

   1. drawing the cone, sundae dish and banana split dish;

   2. how to make Ice Cream Treats.

2. Child draws:

a. cone on 3" x 3":

   1. draw diagonal line from top center to bottom corner;

   2. repeat for second line of cone from top center to opposite bottom corner.

b. sundae dish on 3" x 3" draw as for cone;

c. banana split dish on 2" x 6":

   1. draw 6" line across the bottom of the rectangle;

   2. draw 6" line across the top of the rectangle;

   3. draw an angled line from the top corner of rectangle to bottom of rectangle;

   4. draw an angled line from opposite top corner of rectangle to bottom of rectangle.

3. Child cuts:

a. lines on 3" x 3" into drawn triangles for cone and sundae dish;

b. lines on 2" x 6" into drawn trapezoid for banana split dish;

c. 1" x 6" into banana;

d. 3" x 3" into circles for ice cream scoops;

e. scraps into:

   1. base for sundae dish;

   2. cherries for toppings;

   3. sprinkles for toppings.

4. set up for gluing; glue:

a. sundae dish to background paper; ice cream to sundae;

b. cone to background paper; ice cream to cone;

c. banana split dish to background paper; banana to dish; ice cream to banana;

d. sprinkles and cherries to ice cream.

5. Clean up (except for crayons/markers).

Stand Up Animal

Supplies

Scissors
Glue
Paper Towels
Newsprint
Pencils/Crayons/Markers
Scrap Box

Teacher-Prepared Materials

Paper Square, 6" x 6" fold to 3" x 6"
(Animal Body) (Child's name on back.)
Paper Square, 3" x 3" (Animal Head)
Paper Scraps, (Additional Animal Parts)

Procedure

1. Small group discussion.
   a. Talk about animals; have pictures and models.
   b. Talk about and demonstrate how to draw the line to make the animal's legs and stomach.
   c. Talk about each piece of paper and what it could become.
   d. Pass out scissors, newsprint and Teacher- Prepared Materials.
   e. Let children tell you about:
      1. drawing the line to make the legs and stomach;
      2. how to make a Stand-Up Animal;
      3. what they will use from the Scrap Box;
      4. what they will make.

2. Child draws line for legs and stomach.

3. Child cuts:
   a. line for legs and stomach:
      1. shape to animal body;
      2. slot on fold to insert head and tail.
   b. 3" x 3" into animal head;
   c. scraps into additional parts.

4. Lay out Stand-up Animal.

5. Set up for gluing; glue:
   a. head to body;
   b. tail to body;
   c. additional parts to body;
   d. items from the scrap box.

6. Clean up.

Note: Children may create independent ideas with these materials.

165

Stuffed Paper Bag Puppet

Supplies

Scissors
Glue
Paper Towels
Small Paper Bag
Empty Toilet Paper Roll
1 Sheet of Newsprint (stuff bag)
Newsprint (practice drawing)
Pencils/Crayons/Markers
Cellophane Tape
Scrap Box

Teacher-Prepared Materials

Paper Strip, 1 1/2" x 8" (Eyes, Nose, Mouth)
Paper Rectangle, 5" x 8" (Hair)
Scrap Paper

Procedure

1. Small group discussion.
a. Talk about puppets; talk about imagination.
b. Talk about the pieces to be used to make this puppet.
c. Tell children the project will be made in a different sequence than other projects.
2. Make Puppet base.
a. Pass out paper bags, newsprint, and toilet paper rolls;
b. child stuffs paper bag with newsprint;
c. child/teacher tapes stuffed paper bag on to toilet paper roll.
3. Learn to draw zig-zag lines.
a. talk about zig-zagged lines;
b. pass out newsprint and crayon/marker;
c. child practices drawing zig-zagged lines on newsprint.
4. Talk about and demonstrate how to complete the puppet.
5. Let children tell you about:
a. zig-zagged lines;
b. how to complete this puppet.
6. Child cuts and draws:
a. cuts 5" x 8" into 8" strips:
1. draws zig-zagged lines onto strips;
2. cuts on zig-zagged lines.
b. folds 1 1/2" x 8" in half:
1. cut on fold;
2. fold 1 1/2" X 4" in half;
3. cut on fold;
4. draw eyes, nose, mouth on pieces;
5. cut out eyes, nose and mouth.
c. cut scraps into additional desired pieces.
7. Lay out puppet.
8. Set up for gluing; glue:
a. hair to bag;
b. face to bag;
c. additional pieces to bag.
9. Clean up.

Note: Children may create independent ideas with these materials.

Children's Ideas

Children's Ideas

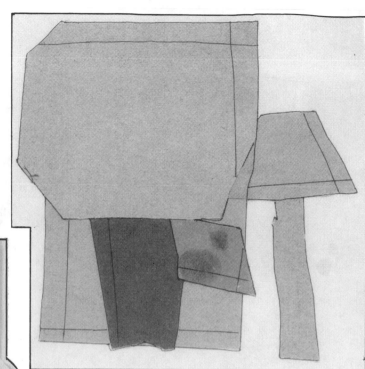

168

Teacher Ideas

1. See Free Cutting Sides and Angles.
2. Television Set.
3. Put out templates (square, rectangle, hexagon, triangle), shapes from packing cartons (only if shipping non-toxic items). Encourage your children to use markers, pencils or crayons to draw the shapes, then cut them out. The drawing and cutting may be all some of the children are interested in. Others may want glue and other items to "make something." Encourage them to create their own ideas.
4. Give the child a 5" x 5" square to free-hand draw a square spiral and cut it out. Actually, the drawing of a square spiral will be more difficult than drawing a circular spiral, although the cutting of a circle spiral is more difficult than a square spiral. Some children may want you to draw the square spiral for them. Please do. These same children will love cutting the square spiral.

169

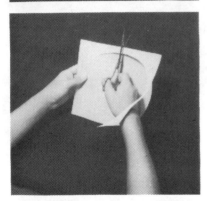

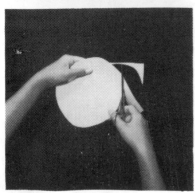

Turning
The Paper For Rounded Shapes And Curves - Line

I. Instructions

NOTE: Turning the paper to free cut a circle is an essential skill, before adding the line. Continue to give the child many experiences with lined curved shapes: walking, drawing, crawling, sorting, finding, building, and talking about circles and ovals. Also give the child instruction and practice time drawing with curved shape templates, before and during this skill.

A. Skill
Positioning a lined curve in relation to the scissors blade. (Turning the paper and cutting was learned during the free cutting sequence.)

B. Language
curved line	circle	oval
round shape	draw inside template	

C. Circle
1. Materials
   a. Paper square
      Not larger than 8" x 8"
      Not smaller than 3" x 3".
   b. Pencils, Crayons, Markers.
   c. Circle template no larger than the size of the paper square.
   d. Clipboard.
   e. Using the template, the child draws a circle about the size of the square.
   f. Also allow the children to draw free-hand circles. (Use paper squares and paper circles for the child to draw on.)
2. Procedure
NOTE: Photos for Free Cutting
   a. Relaxed cutting position.

b. The hands and paper form a straight line parallel to the body. Hand-paper-hand.

c. Cutting begins on the side opposite the paper-holding hand, where the circle is nearest the side of the square.

d. Cut along the curved line towards the top side of square, using a long stroke of the scissors.

e. As the scissors reach the top side, turn the square so that the hanging excess paper can be easily clipped off.

f. Move paper-holding hand towards the body to hold the next side of the square.

g. Hands should now be in the original cutting position. Continue cutting the curve line towards the top side.

h. Repeat the clipping-off of excess paper and the moving of the paper-holding hand.

i. The hands will find a natural rhythm of cutting and turning the square.

j. Continue to cut off the excess paper as needed.

k. Scissors do not close while cutting circle.

l. Scissors may close when clipping off excess and on final snip.

171

m. Verbally label shape as a circle.

D. Oval

1. Materials

a. Paper rectangle.
   Not longer than 8"
   Not wider than 5"

b. Pencils, Crayons or Markers.

c. Template no larger than the size of the paper rectangle.

d. Clipboard.

e. Using the template, the child draws an oval with one edge near the side of the rectangle.

f. Free-hand drawn ovals almost the size of the paper.

2. Procedure

Following instructions for circle, cut out oval.

II. Problems and Solutions

A. Cannot turn and cut at the same time

1. See solutions in free-cutting sequence.

2. Continue to do activities with curved shapes that involve the body.

3. Activities that require each hand to perform a different task.

B. Does not follow the line

2. Give the child a circle drawn on a circle to cut.

3. Return to cutting straight lines.

4. Make visual checks.

5. Provide left-handed scissors for the left-handed child.

Sea Headband

Supplies

Scissors
Glue
Paper Towels
Crayons/Pencils/Markers
Scrap Box

Teacher-Prepared Materials

4 Paper Squares, 3" x 3" (Bodies)
4 Paper Squares, 3" x 3" (Heads)
Paper Strip, 1" x 12" (Eyes, Nose, Mouth)
Paper Rectangle, 4" x 12" (Sea Bottom)
Paper Strip, 6" x 24" (Headband)
   (Child's name on back.)

Procedure

1. *Small group discussion.*
   a. Talk about the sea about and sea animals; have pictures and models;
   b. Talk about and demonstrate drawing curved shapes;
   c. Talk about and demonstrate cutting a curved shape:
      1. turning just the paper while cutting;
      2. keeping the line inside the scissors' blade.
   d. Talk about each piece of paper and demonstrate what it could become;
   e. Pass out scissors and Teacher-Prepared Materials;
   f. Let children tell you about:
      1. drawing curved shapes;
      2. cutting curved shapes;
      3. how to make their Sea Headband;
      4. what they will make.

2. *Child draws:*
   a. a curved line down the center of the 4" x 12" sea bottom;
   b. bodies onto 3"x 3" squares;
   c. heads onto 3" x 3" squares.

3. *Child chooses items from scrap box.*

4. *Child cuts:*
   a. lined 4" x 12" into sea bottom;
   b. lined 3" x 3" into heads and bodies;
   c. scraps into additional pieces.

5. *Lay out Sea Headband.*

6. *Set up for gluing; glue:*
   a. sea bottom on headband;
   b. sea animals in sea;
   c. additional pieces child cut;
   d. items from scrap box.

7. *Clean up.*

8. *Measure headband to fit child's head and staple headband together.*

Note: Children may create independent ideas with these materials.

Sandwich

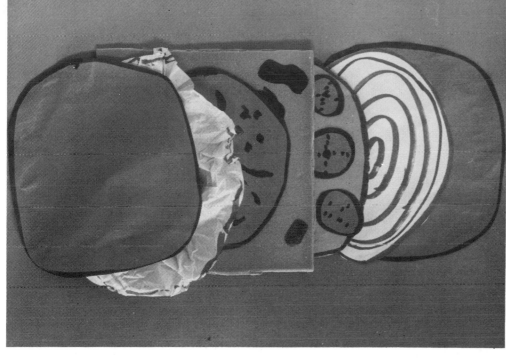

Supplies

Scissors
Glue
Paper Towels
Crayons/Pencils/Markers
5" diameter Circle Template
Clipboard
Scrap Box

Teacher-Prepared Materials

2 Paper Squares, 6" x 6" (Bun)
Tissue Paper Square, 6" x 6" (Lettuce)
Paper Square, 6" x 6" (Tomato)
Styrofoam Square, 6" x 6" (Cheese)
Cardboard Square, 6" x 6" (Meat)
Paper Square, 6" x 6" (Onion)
Paper Strip, 1 1/2" X 4" (Pickles)
Background Paper, 12" x 18"
(Child's name on back.)

Procedure

1. Small group discussion.
a. Talk about sandwiches; how to make them; what children like on them.
b. Talk about and demonstrate how to use a template and clipboard.
c. Circle may be drawn free hand. Talk about and demonstrate how to draw a large circle almost touching each of the sides of the square.
d. Talk about and demonstrate how to cut a curved line.
e. Talk about each piece of paper and demonstrate what it could become.
f. Pass out scissors, clipboards, circle template and Teacher-Prepared Materials.
g. Let children tell you about:
  1. if using template - how to use it;
  2. if drawing free hand - how to draw it;
  3. how to make their Sandwichs;
  4. what they will make.

2. Child draws:
a. circles on all of the squares, except cheese;
b. additional marks on circles to make tomato and onion;
c. holes in cheese
d. circles on 1 1/2" x 4" for pickles, additional markings.

3. Child cuts:
a. lined circles into bun, lettuce; tomato, meat and onion;
b. snip off lined circles on 1 1/2" x 4"; cut circles into pickles.

4. Lay out Sandwich.

5. Set up for gluing; glue:
a. 1/2 bun to background;
b. layer other ingredients;
c. other 1/2 of bun last;
d. additional items from scrap box.

6. Clean up.

Note: Children may create independent ideas with these materials.

173

Cookies

Supplies

Scissors
Glue
Paper Towels
Crayons/Pencils/Markers
Cookie Cutters
Odd Template Shapes
Clipboard
Scrap Box

Teacher-Prepared Materials

A Paper Square or Rectangle For Each Cookie Cutter or Odd Template Shape
Scrap Pieces for Free Hand Drawing
Background paper (Cookie Sheet)
(Child's name on back.)

Procedure

1. Small group discussion.
   a. Talk about making cookies and the shapes cookies might be. "Have samples!"
   b. Talk about and demonstrate how to draw around the outside of the cookie cutter.
   c. Talk about drawing some cookies free hand.
   d. Pass out scissors, crayons, cookie cutters, templates, clipboard and Teacher-Prepared Materials.
   e. Let children tell you about:
      1. drawing around the outside of the cookie cutter;
      2. what they will make;
      3. using templates;
      4. drawing cookies free hand;
      5. how to make their cookies.

2. Child draws cookies:
   a. using cookie cutters;
   b. using odd shape templates;
   c. free hand.
3. Child selects items from scrap box.
4. Child cuts:
   a. lined cookies;
   b. additional decoration from scraps;
5. Lay out Cookie Sheet.
6. Set up for gluing; glue:
   a. Cookies to sheet;
   b. decorations to Cookies.
7. Clean up.

Note: Children may create independent ideas with these materials.

Gumball Machine

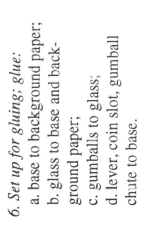

Supplies

Scissors
Glue
Paper Towels
Crayons/Pencils/Markers
7" diameter Circle Template
Clipboard
Scrap Box

Teacher-Prepared Materials

Paper Square, 8" x 8" (Glass)
Paper Strips, 1" x 12" (Gumballs)
Paper Square, 3" x 3" (Base)
Paper Scraps, (Lever, Coin Slot, Gumball Chute)
Background Paper, 12" x 18"
(Child's name on back.)

Procedure

1. Small group discussion.
   a. Talk about gumball machines.
   b. Talk about and demonstrate how to use the templates and clipboard.
   c. Talk about and demonstrate how to draw free hand circles on the strip.
   d. Talk about each piece of paper and demonstrate what it could become.
   e. Pass out scissors, board, template and Teacher-Prepared Materials.
   f. Let children tell you about:
      1. using the template and clipboard;
      2. drawing free hand circles on paper strip;
      3. how to make their Gumball Machine;
      4. what they will make.
2. Child draws:
   a. circle on 8" x 8" (glass);
   b. circles on 1" x 12" strip.
3. Child selects items from scrap box.
4. Child cuts:
   a. lined circle of 8" x 8" for glass;
   b. snips off circles on 1" x 12" strip; cuts lined circles into gum;
   c. scraps into lever, coin slot, gumball chute;
   d. scrap box items.
5. Lay out Gumball Machine.

6. Set up for gluing; glue:
   a. base to background paper;
   b. glass to base and background paper;
   c. gumballs to glass;
   d. lever, coin slot, gumball chute to base.

7. Clean up.

Note: Children may create independent ideas with these materials.

175

Crab

Supplies

Scissors
Glue
Paper Towels
Crayons/Pencils/Markers
Scrap Box

Teacher-Prepared Materials

Paper Rectangle, 2" x 6" (Body)
6 Paper Strips, 1" x 3" (Legs)
2 Paper Strips, 1" x 4" (Claws)
Paper Scrap, (Stalked Eyes)
Background Paper, 9" x 12"
(Child's name on back.)

Procedure

1. *Small group discussion.*
a. Talk about crabs; have pictures.
b. Talk about and demonstrate drawing ovals and egg shapes.
c. Talk about each piece of paper and demonstrate what it will become.
d. Pass out scissors, crayons and Teacher-Prepared Materials.

e. Let children tell you about:
1. drawing ovals and egg shapes;
2. how to make their Crab;
3. what they will make.

2. *Child draws:*
a. crab body on 2" x 6";
b. 3 ovals on 1" x 3" for legs;
c. 3 ovals on 2" x 4" for claws.

3. *Child cuts:*
a. lined crab body;
b. snip lined ovals off strips; cut lined ovals into legs and claws;
c. scraps into stalked eyes.

4. *Lay out Crab.*

5. *Add items from scrap box.*

6. *Set up for gluing; glue:*
a. body to background paper;
b. legs to body and background paper;
c. claws to body and back ground paper;
d. stalked eyes to body.

7. *Clean up.*

Note: Children may create independent ideas with these materials.

Ferris Wheel

Supplies

Scissors
Glue
Paper Towels
Crayons/Pencils/Markers
8" diameter Circle Template
3" diameter Circle Template
Clipboard
Scrap Box

Procedure

1. Small group discussion.

a. Talk about Ferris Wheel; have pictures.

b. Talk about and demonstrate how to use the templates and clipboard.

c. If drawing circles free hand, talk about and demonstrate how to draw a circle almost touches each of the sides of the square.

d. Talk about and demonstrate how to cut a pie shape out of the small circles.

e. Talk about each piece of paper and demonstrate what it could become.

f. Pass out scissors, clipboards, templates and Teacher-Prepared Materials.

g. Let children tell you about:

Teacher-Prepared Materials

Paper Square, 9" x 9" (Wheel)
8 Paper Squares, 4" x 4" (Seats)
Paper Strip, 1 1/2" x 12" (Heads)
Paper Rectangle, 3" x 5" (Base)
Background Paper, 9" x 12" (Child's name on back.)

1. using the templates and clipboard;
2. drawing a circle free hand;
3. cutting a pie shape out of the seat circles;
4. how to make their Ferris Wheel.

2. Child draws:

a. circle on 9" x 9" square (wheel);
b. circles on 4" x 4" squares (seats);
c. circles on 1 1/2" x 12" strip (heads).

3. Child cuts:

a. lined circle on 9" x 9" for wheel;
b. lined circle on 4" x 4"; pie shape out of each circle for seats;
c. snip off lined circles on 1 1/2" x 12"; cut lined circles into heads;

d. diagonal strips off of 3" x 5" for base.

4. Lay out Ferris Wheel.

5. Set up for gluing; glue:

a. base to bottom of background paper;
b. wheel to base and background paper;

c. seats to wheel;
d. head to wheel circles on 1 1/2" x 12" strip (heads).

6. Clean up (except for crayons/markers).

7. Child adds drawings to project.

Note: Children may create independent ideas with these materials.

177

Children's Ideas

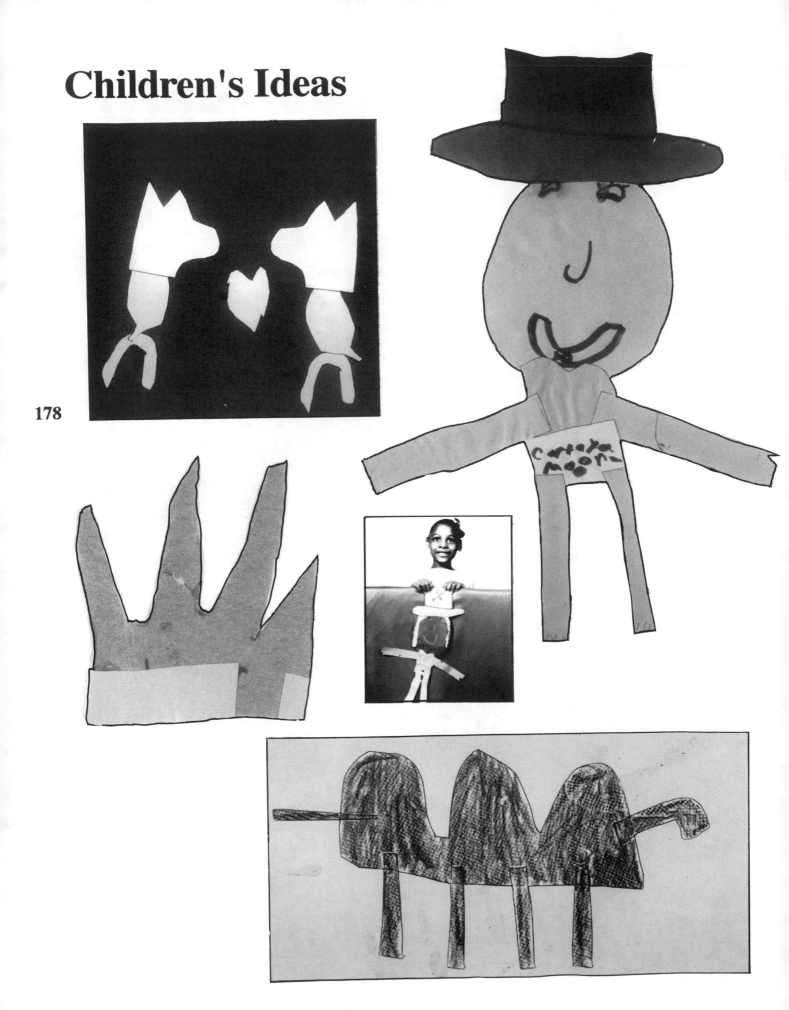

Children's Ideas

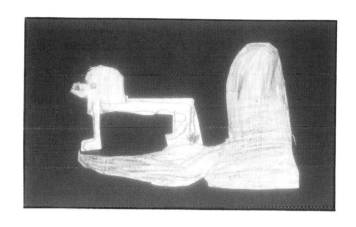

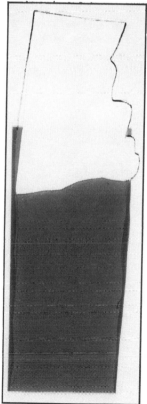

Teacher Ideas

1. Provide paper circles with circles drawn on them.
2. Put out many pre-cut rounded shapes and encourage your children to use them.
3. Make 10" diameter circles available. Talk about drawing a spiral free-hand and how to cut it out.
4. Draw wavy lines on strips of paper.
5. Provide blank strips for the children to draw their own wavy lines and cut.
6. Encourage children to move the paper strip to free cut wavy lines.

A Final Note...

Your children now have the basic skills they need to move on to complex cutting. Now that they realize they can move the paper around to create many kinds of shapes, they will please themselves, and you, with their creations.

Continue to value free cutting because it will allow for the widest range of creativity from your children. Encourage your children to fold the paper and cut. Help them to experiment with cutting and leaving the fold

180 uncut.

Believe in the independent creation of your children and you will all have fun cutting up!

Multi-Use Guide to Activities

Bug Headband, 102

Ferris Wheel, 177

Birthday Hat, 118

As your children learn to cut and you become more familiar with the sequence of **Children and Scissors**, you will find that you and your children will begin to use your creative energies to create all kinds of interesting activities.

To help you to use this book creatively, this multi-use guide suggests a wide range of ways to include the activities in your curriculum planning.

Use the guide to find the activity you need. Then you can adapt it to the current cutting skills of your children in three ways:

● If the activity is **beyond** the child's skill level:
  Pre-cut the more difficult pieces.
  Example: The children are snipping. They can make the Stick Puppet at Thanksgiving if you pre-cut the advanced pieces.

● If the activity is **at** the child's skill level:
  Congratulate yourself on good timing.
  Do the activity more than once.
  Alter the activity.
  Example: Make the Bear into a Cat by adding a tail and pointed ears.

● If the activity is **below** the child's skill level:
  Do it again to reinforce skills already learned.
  Give lots of room for creative expression. Pass out extra scrap paper.
  Example: See how many kinds of Flowers they can make.

* Allow children to create their own ideas with the materials you give them.

181

Animals / Zoo

Baby Bird in Nest, 139
Bear, 20
Butterfly, 13
Crab, 176
Creepy Animal, 60
Elephant, 92
Fish, 38
Frog, 116
Giraffe, 140
Horse's Head, 130
Lamb, 105
Lion in a Cage, 151
Lion's Face, 49
Octopus, 115
Owl, 51
Peacock, 95
Pig, 117
Porcupine, 50
Small Creature, 72
Snail, 63
Snake, 133
Stand-up Animal, 165
Turtle, 94
Underwater Mobile, 107
Wiggle Creature, 81

American Indians

Bear, 20
Fish, 38
Headbands, 40, 48, 70, 80, 128, 138
Hopi Kachina, 52
Necklace, 39
Porcupine, 50
Stick Puppet, 75
Stand-Up Animal, 165

Birthday

Birthday Hat, 118
Headbands, 11, 40, 48, 70, 80, 128, 138, 149, 161, 172

Alligator, 141

182

Necklace, 39

Giraffe, 140

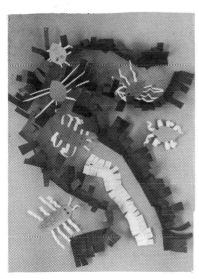

Bugs in Grass, 142

Fringed Headband, 48

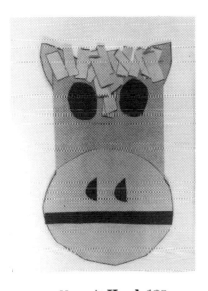

Horse's Head, 130

183

Further Readings

Child Development

Cherry, Clare, *Creative Art for the Developing Child,* Lear Siegler Inc./Fearon Publishers, Belmont, California, 1972.

Erhardt, Rhoda, *Sequential Levels in Development of Prehension,* American Journal of Occupational Therapy, Vol. 28, No. 10, Nov.-Dec. 1974.

Gesell, A., *Developmental Diagnosis,* Holber Medical Division, Harper & Row, New York, 1969.

Kohl, Mary Ann, *Mud Works,* Ring Publishers, Billingham, Washington, 1989.

Moll, Patricia Buerke, *Children & Books I,* Hampton Mae Institute, Tampa, Florida, 1994.

Piaget, J., *The Origins of Intelligence in Children,* International Universal Press, New York, 1952.

Nursery Rhymes / Folk Lore / Fairytales

Field, Edward, *Eskimo Songs & Stories,* Dell Publishing, 1973.

Greenfield, Eloise, *Honey I Love,* Harper Collins, New York, 1978.

Griego, Margot C., et al, *Tortillitas Para Mama and other Spanish Nursery Rhymes,* Henry Holt & Co., New York, 1981.

Hamilton, Virginia, *The People Could Fly,* American Black Folk Tales, Alfred A. Knopf, New York, 1985.

Haviland, Virginia, *Favorite Fairy Tales,* (many countries), Little Brown and Company, Boston, 1963 to present.

Hitz, Demi, *Dragon Kites and Dragonflies,* A Collection of Chinese Nursery Rhymes, Harcourt Brace Jovanovich, Inc., Orlando, FL, 1986.

Latham, Hugh, *Mother Goose in French,* Thomas Y. Crowell Company, New York.

McDermott, Gerald, *Anansi the Spider,* Holt, Rinehart & Winston, New York, 1972.

Medearis, Angela Shelf, *Dancing with the Indians,* Holiday, Chicago, 1993.

Michels, Barbara and Bettye White, *Apples On A Stick, The Folklore of Black Children*, Coward-McCann, Inc., New York, 1983.

Montgomerie, Norak and William, *Scottish Nursery Rhymes,* Oxford University Press, New York, 1965.

Reid, Alastair, *Mother Goose in Spanish,* Thomas Y. Crowell Company, New York, 1968.

Wood, Ray, *Fun in American Folk Rhymes,* J.B. Lippincott Co., Philadelphia.

Wright, Blanche Fisher, *The Real Mother Goose,* Rand McNally and Co., Chicago, 1944.

Wyndham, Robert, *Chinese Mother Goose Rhymes,* The World Publishing Company, Cleveland, Ohio 44102, 1968.

Paper Crafts

Borja, Robert & Corinne, *Making Chinese Paper Cuts,* Albert Witman & Co., Chicago, 1980.

Brown, Jerome C., *Folk Tale Paper Crafts,* Fearon, Mother Goose Paper Crafts, New York, 1989.

Comins, Jeremy, *Slotted Sculpture from Cardboard,* Lothrop, Lee & Shepard, New York, 1977.

Grater, Michael, *Paper Play,* Milles & Bloom Ltd., London, 1972.

Grol, Lini, *Scissorcraft,* Sterling Publishing Co., Inc., New York, 1970.

Hou-tien Ching, *Scissor Cutting for Beginners,* Holt, Rinehart & Winston, NY, 1978.

Huff, Vivian, *Let's Make Paper Dolls,* Harper and Row Publishers, NY, 1978.

Irvine, Joan, *How to Make Pop-Ups,* Morrow Junior Books, New York, 1987.

Matisse, Henri, *Jazz* V.A.G.A., New York, 1983.

Temko, Florence, *Paper Cutting,* Doubleday and Company, Inc., Garden City, New York, 1973.

West, Robin, *Paper Circus,* Carolrhoda Books, Inc., Minneapolis, 1983.

Woods, Pamela, *Papercraft,* St. Martins Press, New York, 1980.

Zarchy, Harry, *Papercraft,* World Publishing Co., New York, 1966.

Scissoring Skills Mastery Record - Free Cutting - 1

NAME _____

DATE STARTED _____

	Introduced	Learning	Acquired
I. Glue			
Finger paints with glue and paste			
Uses large quantity of glue and paste			
Uses whole hand to spread glue or paste			
Uses fingers to spread glue or paste			
Uses one finger to spread glue or paste			
Uses appropriate quantity of glue and paste			
II. Tear			
Hands pull away from mid-line to make tear			
Hands pull away from and toward body to make short tear			
Hands pull away from and toward body to make long tear			
III. Snip			
Scissor Manipulation (opens and closes)			
Holds paper/scissors at 90° angle			
Uses standard scissors grip			
Opening strength			
Closing strength			
Uses full length of scissors blade			
Relaxed cutting posture			
IV. Fringe			
Stopping scissoring action near end of blade			
Uses almost the full length of scissors blade			
Relaxed cutting posture			
V. Strip			
Moves scissors through a length of paper			
Holds paper with scissor blades			
Moves paper, holding hand in rhythm with scissors			
Uses almost the full length of scissors blade			
Relaxed cutting position			

185

DATE COMPLETED _____

Reprinted by permission from *Children and Scissors* © Patricia B. Moll, 4104 Lynn Avenue, Tampa, Florida 33603.

Scissoring Skills Mastery Record - Free Cutting - 2

NAME_____

DATE STARTED_____

	Introduced	Learning	Acquired
VI. Sides			
Cut off paper side			
Turn paper to cut off an additional side			
Uses almost full length of scissors blade			
Relaxed cutting posture			
VII. Angles			
Stop cutting in middle of paper			
Turn paper, position scissors, cut			
Uses almost the full length of scissors blade			
Relaxed cutting posture			
VIII. Turning the Paper for Rounded Shapes			
Turn the paper and cut at the same time			
Uses almost the full length of scissors blade			
Relaxed cutting posture			
IX. Curves			
Turn paper and cut at the same time			
Move paper-holding hand and scissors in a natural rhythm to cut curves			
End curve where cutting began			
Uses almost the full length of scissors blade			
Relaxed cutting posture			
X. Spiral			
Cuts spiral			
Uses almost the full length of scissors blade			
Relaxed cutting position			

DATE COMPLETED _____

Reprinted by permission from *Children and Scissors* © Patricia B. Moll, 4104 Lynn Avenue, Tampa, Florida 33603.

Scissoring Skills Mastery Record - Line Cutting - 3

NAME_____

DATE
STARTED_____

	Introduced	Learning	Acquired
I. Snip-Line			
Placement of scissors in relation to the lines			
Relaxed cutting position			
Uses almost the full length of scissors blade			
II. Fringe-Line			
Stopping scissor action at end of line			
Relaxed cutting position			
Uses almost the full length of scissors blade			
III. Strip-Line			
Move scissors following a line			
Relaxed cutting position			
Uses almost the full length of scissors blade			
IV. Sides and Angles-Line			
Positioning a lined angle in relation to the scissors blade			
Relaxed cutting position			
Uses almost the full length of scissors blade			
V. Turning the Paper for Rounded Shapes and Curved-Lines			
Position a lined curve in relation to the scissors blade			
Turn the paper while cutting beside a line			
Relaxed cutting position			
Uses almost the full length of scissors blade			

187

DATE COMPLETED _____

Reprinted by permission from *Children and Scissors* © Patricia B. Moll, 4104 Lynn Avenue, Tampa, Florida 33603.

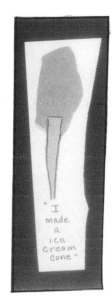

"I made a ice cream cone"

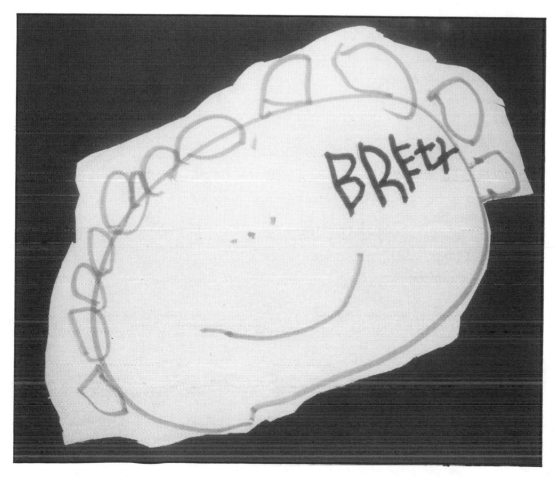

BREtt

Children & Books I
African American Story Books and Activities for All Children

Second Edition

This book introduces you to the best of 86 children's story books featuring Black children from America, England and Africa as main characters. Moll has selected 25 new books for the Second Edition. The story books were written or illustrated by African-Americans, or are about African culture, customs and folklore. In addition, authors and illustrators of African heritage who live in England, Kenya and South Africa are included. Moll has suggestions for the presentation of each book and follow-up activities for use throughout the curriculum.

Children & Scissors
A Developmental Approach

Third Edition

Thirteen sequential steps for learning the art of cutting, including gluing, pasting, free cutting and line cutting, are presented. Common problems are identified and classroom-tested solutions are suggested. There are 88 sequential cut and paste activities which are open-ended and guide teachers to encourage children to explore with their materials. The book gives instructions for teachers on developmental growth through process and while encouraging children to control and define their own product.

Contact your local School Supply Dealer, Children's Bookstore   **or call or write:**   **Patricia B. Moll**
4104 Lynn Avenue
Tampa, Florida 33603-3421
(813) 238-2221

Clip And Return To Patricia Buerke Moll 4104 Lynn Avenue Tampa, FL 33603-3421

Yes, I'm interested in:

☐ buying copies of *Children & Books I* and *Children & Scissors* for a total price of **$25.00**, plus **$3.50** for postage and handling.

☐ buying ___ copies/copy of ___*Children & Books I* or ___ *Children & Scissors* for a price of **$14.95** each, plus **$2.50** for postage and handling for each book.

    Enclosed is my check for $_____.____.

Name:_____   Ship To:_____

Address:_____   Address:_____

City:_____ State:____ Zip:_____   City:_____ State:____ Zip:_____

Your Daytime Phone: (___)_____   Your Evening Phone (___)_____

○ Please send me information about your workshop & training presentations.

○ Please send me your price list for the books featured in *Children & Books I*.